MY BREAST CANCER ORDEAL

A Miracle Journey How God Strength Was Made Perfect In My Weakness.

NICOLE LINESZY

Copyright © 2016 by Nicole Lineszy

My Breast Cancer Ordeal
A Miracle Journey How God Strength Was Made Perfect In My Weakness.
by Nicole Lineszy

Printed in the United States of America.

ISBN 9781498493567

All rights reserved solely by the author. The author guarantees all contents are original and do not infringe upon the legal rights of any other person or work. No part of this book may be reproduced in any form without the permission of the author. The views expressed in this book are not necessarily those of the publisher.

www.xulonpress.com

TABLE OF CONTENTS

Happiness Interrupted 7
Acceptance 15
Action 18
Joy 25
Back To Reality 29
The Battle Zone 52
Reflections 61
Reality 62
Empowerment 63
Radiation Therapy 68
Free At Last 74
My Rebirth 74
Disappointment 79
Transformation 85
Special Thanks 91

HAPPINESS INTERRUPTED

When I was diagnosed with cancer in 2010, I was still enjoying newly-wedded bliss. I had recently married a wonderful man, Alton Lineszy, and moved into a new apartment. We did everything that married couples do, including going out to dinner on the weekends or just having a movie night at our house with pop corn and soda. I was very active in my local church and obedient to the word of God to live a good Christian life. A cancer diagnosis was the last thing I expected to hear. No one in my family ever had cancer so the thought never entered my mind. Besides, I was only 38 years old. I could not possibly have breast cancer. However I was dead wrong. I sat in my doctor's office and heard what no woman wants to hear. I had breast Cancer. This is the story of my ordeal and how the goodness of God begins.

One morning, I felt a lump in my right breast. I thought it was nothing and that it would go away however, It never did. Instead, it kept getting bigger and bigger, harder and harder. I even monitored it to see if it had something to do with my menstrual cycle. When I finally decided to see my gynecologist, she gave me a mammogram referral. I had never had one done before. The appointment was in two weeks. Everyday I would feel my breast, hoping the lump would disappear on its own. But it was still there growing inside of me, feeding off my body's nutrients. I was comforted by the fact that the lump was painless and my nipple did not leak, yet I was desperate to know the cause of this rapid growth in my breast. I hoped desperately that a few antibiotics would make it disappear. I realized that the hardest thing for a person to do is to wait on a doctor's report, knowing that there was the possibility of a diagnosis that you didn't want to hear.

The morning of my mammogram I prayed and ask God to please let everything be alright. I prayed that the report would be all good and there would be nothing to worry about. The process of the test was much more intense than I anticipated. I wondered how women endured such excruciating pain every year. I can only compare the pain to that of giving birth but in a different part of my body. The test was over and I was happy to leave the examination room with my breasts. I was told that my doctor would get the results in two weeks.

I went about life as usual. I kept busy because it was Christmas time and there were a lot of preparations to be made at my apartment. I have always continued in the traditions of my native country, Trinidad and Tobago. Installing curtain rods, hanging up curtains, mounting pictures on the wall and arranging furniture. Shopping for Christmas decorations and food for guests, are still is my favorite holiday activity.

Two weeks later, I was back at my doctor's office for the test results. While she sat at her desk reading the computer screen, her facial expression told me that something was wrong. She turned to me and said, "Sorry, but your test came back abnormal; you would need further testing." Further testing meant a sonogram (It is more accurate than a mammogram). As the doctor tried to explain things to me my tears kept flowing. I tried to keep myself as calm as possible, that I would not miss anything that was important. In the ten years that I have known my doctor, I never saw her so uncomfortable. I knew that things were not good.

My doctor asked several questions, such as -: Was there anyone in my family with breast cancer? How old was I when I first started having my menstrual cycle? Did I breast feed my daughter; For how long? I started menstruating at age twelve, and no, I did not breast feed my daughter. The doctor scheduled the sonogram appointment for the earliest available date- one month away. I needed to have the test done immediately but there were no earlier dates. I went home that afternoon feeling very disappointed with myself for not taking action sooner. All I could do at that moment was to pray.

The sonogram was very relaxing compared to the mammogram. In about thirty minutes, I was up and out of the examination room. The results showed that there were several lumps of different sizes, although I only felt one that is when I started to get scared. Again, my doctor recommended further testing–this time, a needle biopsy. A needle biopsy is done by testing a sample of the affected area for possible cancer. I was scheduled immediately.

The morning of the biopsy I was a little nervous, because I did not know exactly what to expect, but the nurse made me feel as comfortable as possible. She explained the procedure and told me that everything would take about thirty to forty five minutes but first, the doctor wanted to repeat the sonogram so that she could pinpoint the exact position of the lumps. During the procedure, I could hear the nurse and the doctor describing the positions of the lumps as seven o'clock and eleven o'clock. I never knew that they described the positions as if they were looking at a clock. After my biopsy was over, I felt sore for days. I wished I didn't feel this way since there was not much I could have done during the holidays with a sore breast.

All the same, the holiday season was wonderful. My husband and I visited friends and family and I did not pay any attention to my health or to my father, who had suffered a stroke two weeks earlier. I kept my focus on having an enjoyable holiday. Nevertheless, on January 1st, my daughter called and said that my father had just died. Although I knew that my father had been a diabetic for a long time, I hoped that he would get over and be well. Sadly, the stroke had done a lot of damage to his brain and there was not much the doctors could have done to save him. He was sixty five years old, which I considered to be young. He was the best father, a loving husband, great grandfather and generous friend. I missed talking to him so much at times, I consoled myself in knowing that God knows best.

After the holidays, I was back at the hospital to get the results of the biopsy. I had strong faith that morning that all would be well but I was in for a shock. The doctor said that I had cancer in my right breast. I could not believe what I had just heard, I was furious. How could this have happened? It was impossible for me to have cancer. The biopsy must have lied. The doctor took a long time to explain the diagnosis to me. I had DCIS, or Ductal Carcinoma In Situ, it is the most noninvasive type of breast cancer which was supposed to be good news to me. It was at an early stage and could be taken care of. But how could that be good news to me? A cancer diagnosis, whether early or not, is what anyone wants to hear. Not even for your worst enemy. That's like reading a death sentence to someone. As I sat in the chair, I felt like I was sinking. I started to feel sick in my stomach. This was not happening. Somebody please pinch me, wake me up from this horrible nightmare. Cancer? No way, not me, not in this lifetime, I started to go into a trance. I felt like I was in another world because the doctor was talking and my mind was completely somewhere else. Then I remembered that at church, many times my pastor asked "Whose report do you believe?" This time I wanted to believe the report of the Lord. I felt as if life had been knocked right out of me, I was weak, I was in shock. Could I have done something to prevent this or had I done something wrong in my life to deserve this? Was cancer going to take me out? I needed my husband. We had confidence that the report would have been good so there was no need for him to take a day from work to come with me. Now I was longing for him just to hold me in his arms and say, "It's all right, baby, we're going to fight this." But he was not with me. So I comforted myself by clinging tightly to my pocket book. I was afraid that it would walk away and leave me.

Suddenly, I had gone from being happy to being depressed. I tried to snap back to reality but I could not. The thought of Cancer having a strong hold on me I could not break myself free. The doctor kept on asking if everything was alright. How in hell could everything be alright when you told me I have cancer? I wanted to scream but I was afraid to make a commotion. Maybe I would feel better, but I told myself they would think that I am crazy. It doesn't matter how strong someone is, there are some news that can be very heart breaking and devastating. In times like this some people may question God because they aren't aware of the solutions to life's problems. The doctor suggested that I have the surgery as soon as possible. Therefore, I was scheduled in less than two weeks. I tried to explain that my father just died and I would like to leave the country for a short time. However, he insisted that my father was already dead and if I didn't want to be next I should have the surgery done without delay. Although I wanted to be with my mother in this grievous situation, I went with the doctor's advice. I had to go along with the doctor. I had to have a pretest one week before surgery.

The moment I left the doctor's office I broke down in tears. This time my husband was on the other end of the phone. He was in shock and kept asking if I was sure that the doctor said I had breast cancer. He was scared. I could tell from his tone of voice. Then he said what I had been longing to hear. "Everything will be alright. Baby, don't worry." He knew that I had been dealing with a lot. First, my brother's death, then my father's, and now this. But I wanted to go to work because I thought that it would be better if I kept myself busy rather than go home to sit around and cry.

As I walked the streets I closed my eyes tightly at times to prevent the tears from flowing. I kept telling myself," This, too, shall pass."The second person I called was my friend Michelle, she said "don't worry, stop crying God is in control and everything is going to be alright". I felt a tiny relief to hear that God was with me and that He knew exactly how I was feeling. He was the one that would give me all of the comfort. He was the one that would heal my body from this disease. That is what He does, that is His specialty. When I arrived on the job, I did everything that I was supposed to do. I tried to keep as calm as possible so that there wouldn't be any unnecessary questions. As the day went by my mind kept on repeating "You have Breast Cancer," It was unbelievable. Those were the words that kept ringing in my ears. My husband called me every few minutes to make sure that I was alright. How I wished that it was all a dream that I would wake up and everything would just go away.

I left work at about 6.00 that evening. It seemed like a very long day to me. I just wanted to be home, away from the public eye. As I sat on the train trying to stay focused, the tears kept coming so I closed my eyes. I didn't want anyone to noticed that something was wrong with me. When I finally got home, my husband was waiting for me right at the front door. He embraced me with a hug and a gentle kiss. He kept saying that everything was going to be alright. He said, "I am here for you and with you ". I cried much harder than before I was letting it all out. I kept wondering how I was going to tell my mother the news. She just buried my father and my brother a little over a year ago. She could not bear to hear more bad news. I was not ready to tell her or my daughter this kind of news. The thought of leaving them out devastated me because I really thought that Cancer meant the end of my life.

My husband and I did not eat dinner that night. We didn't have an appetite. We lost our desire for food. Instead our appetite for God grew. We both got down on our knees and prayed to the Heavenly Father. We needed God in this; He was the only one that could fix our problem. I never heard my husband pray so fervently before, not even when his mom passed a little over a year ago. He asked God to please heal his wife because he wanted me around. He was fighting back the tears. His hands were clasped over his face and his voice was very shaky. After we prayed, we laid in bed cuddling tightly in silence, afraid that one of us might be snatched away. I thought about the happy times before cancer and how the news would affect my mother. Hurting her was the last thing I wanted. I knew that if I were to tell her that I had cancer she probably ends up depressed. I love my mother so much and the secrecy was destroying me. However I had to do what I thought was best for her. I longed for her love and support.

I thought that if my brother was still alive he would have advised me best. Then I thought about my father. What would he have done after hearing that his little angel was diagnosed with breast cancer? Although my husband was right at my side, I still missed my father and my brother deeply. It hurt so much. Two important men in my life. Why were they snatched away from me so early? My brother's murder still haunts me every day of my life. In like, everyone experiences up's and down's I was in a down time and I needed the support of my whole family. However they were all too far away either in another country or living in another state. I was in my weakest moment, I could not function, the diagnosis really hit me hard. At times I would burst into tears, I could not believe the report. No one but God knew exactly how I was feeling; nothing seemed to matter anymore. All the dreams I had for my life began to fade before me. I had no answers because all I was focused on was how I was going to function in the days to come. I am a strong believer in God but my diagnosis knocked my socks off my feet. All I knew about cancer was that it could be fatal and that was all I kept my mind on. My mind was working like a switch, one minute I would be positive, the next fear would over take me and the negative came right in. As I laid in bed, I continued to talk to God because I needed to keep a positive attitude for all the days ahead, I wanted to be a winner. Although your family and friends are praying for a miracle, you the victim must want to win the battle that came to short circuit your life. Cancer is not our friend, it is our enemy.

Then I looked at my husband lying next to me. I wondered how he was really handling all of this. I know that he was trying to be strong for me but at the same time I could tell that he was worried. Men are so good at keeping their emotions under control. However we show our emotions without shame, no one knows how they are really hurting inside. Alton must have called his family and told them what was happening because they all called that night to give their love and to say that everything was going to be just fine. After I settled myself that night, I called my pastor, he prayed with me, he is a very powerful Man of God, and like everyone else, he said that everything was going to be just fine. Before going to bed that night, I prayed a second time asking God to please let me live through this ordeal. I begged of Him to let me live because I was not ready to leave my loved ones. Besides I had not fulfilled my destiny and my purpose, right there and then I knew how precious life was. The prayer that came out of my mouth that night, the desperation to live, to be healthy again, shaped my reality. I pleaded with God to heal my body. I asked him not to let cancer win, I wanted to be the winner. I wanted all of my emotional pain to go away I wanted the strength to fight the disease and be the over- comer. My body was exhausted that night, it was very hard for me to fall asleep. I kept on turning and tossing, and every once in a while my husband would ask if everything was alright, I would nod my head and say yes to him, however, that was not true. The desire to live had made me desperate that night. Maybe it was hard for my husband to sleep too, but he did not say and I did not bother to ask him, I was too caught up in my own emotions. I finally did fall asleep but I got up in the middle of the night to face my thoughts all over again. I wished that my ordeal was just a nightmare; that I'll go to sleep and when I awake cancer would be gone however; it was now my reality. I woke up the next morning and breast cancer woke up with me because it was still a part of me, it had not gone anywhere. It was right there torturing me, I wished that I could have squeezed it out through my nipples, But it was not that simple I would have to go through surgery to remove my breast or the lump and I hated it.

ACCEPTANCE

The next morning, new thoughts were waiting to haunt me, I was told yesterday that I had breast cancer. What was I going to do? I kept asking myself if this was something that was inherited from one of my grandparents, I needed some answers. I called my aunt who lived in New Jersey, since I obviously could not ask my mother. My aunt assured me that Cancer was not in the family. Then I thought what if it had come from my father side of the family? I will never know because of the fact that my father had just died a few weeks earlier and there were no other family members left besides me and my daughter. I needed to tell my daughter what was happening, she lives in Trinidad with my mother. While I was talking to her on the phone about my health, my eyes were filled with tears. I became very emotional from hearing her voice on the other end of the phone. It brought home the fear that I might never hear my child's voice ever again. I tried my very best to keep calm, I knew that I could not relay that fear to her upsetting her was the last thing I wanted, so I kept the hurt to myself. During our conversation, we both agreed that it was not a good idea to tell my mother. After we hung up the phone, I kept wondering if I had done the right thing by telling my daughter about my diagnosis since she was in school preparing for her exams. She was stronger than I thought; she did not break down into tears which I felt very good about. The encouragement I got from her was amazing. Her words to me were "Stay strong and focused." Imagine hearing those words from your twenty -year -old daughter who has just learned that her mother has breast cancer. You would think that she would be weak and hysterical. She was the complete opposite and it satisfied me to know that she took it well. She is the strong one in the family; she makes a difference in our lives. She was there for her grandmother in her time of sorrow and was there consoling me in my time of need.

As the days went by, I felt empty inside. I was not taking part in the affairs of life. I showed no interest in television, or talking on the phone with my friends. My appetite had gone and I had no desire for food or anything, I was still going through denial.

That Sunday, I decided to let my church family know what was happening, so I made an announcement exposing my diagnosis. I told everyone that I had been diagnosed with breast cancer and I was scared for my life, I was shaking during the announcement. I cried, feeling sorry for myself but I knew that I had done the right thing in letting the church know. They all knew about my father and my brother. They had given their support then and I knew that they would be there for me even more at this point in my life. After church, everyone gave me hugs, kisses and words of encouragement. Some were truly saddened to know that I was diagnosed with breast cancer; they all offered to help in whatever way they could. It felt good to know that they all cared and said that I would always be in their prayers I knew that I could rely on them for support. It gave me a sense of comfort to know that I was not alone disclosing my diagnosis brought my best feelings since I received the news, after talking with my church family, I felt a settled in my spirit.

A few days later the hospital called to inform me about the arrangements for my pretest, the nurse gave specific instructions. If I was on any medications, I should bring them with me on the day of the appointment. I was going to have a lumpectomy to remove the cancer cells. This operation is considered breast conserving surgery because only the malignant tumor and the surrounding margin of normal breast tissues are removed. If there were any lymph nodes in the armpit the doctors will also remove those, I did not have any lymph nodes which was another good sign for me. Surgery involving anesthesia can be nerve racking for anyone. The morning of my pretest I was very calm and in good spirits, the nurses were all very

Acceptance

friendly they made me feel as comfortable as possible. They gave a word of encouragement in the examination room. The nurse took a few samples of my blood along with an EKG test. Next, the doctor came in and explained to me the procedure of the lumpectomy. He said that it is an in and out surgery, meaning that I would be discharged once I felt well enough. No overnight stay was necessary. I was surprised to know that a patient admitted for cancer surgery would not be kept overnight, he said that there was no need to worry because I was in good hands.

A few minutes after he left, the anesthesiologist came in and explained his part of the job which was putting me to sleep on the day of the surgery. After all the testing and consulting with the different doctors, my husband and I left the hospital and headed home. I was ready for the surgery because I wanted it to be over, after surgery, the next step would be treatment. As I prepared myself for the day of the surgery, I did a lot of praying. I wanted to have clarity concerning the whole process so that it no longer had a toll on me. I wanted to be set free, I hated mentioning that I was sick even though I was not physically challenged in anyway. I took care of all of my needs on my own. I refuse to put myself in the category of being sick. When someone has cancer it does not matter who you are, the response that you get from the people around you are pitiful. Many times I was asked to attend support groups with patients like myself, but I refused to believe that it would be a sad experience to sit in a room with people expressing their negative emotions. I thought to myself that people who are in support groups are the weak ones and I did not want to put myself in an environment like that but I was wrong. Support groups are for people to express their feelings, and for the over comers who are now in remission to share their story. They encouraged the newly diagnosed patients to have a positive attitude and gave us a sense of hope.

ACTION

The surgery was a week away. While I waited for that day and time to come, I did a lot of research on my own to know more about this horrible disease. While researching, I found that there were many women who survived after they had a lumpectomy with a little radiation, or chemotherapy or maybe both. The thought of having chemotherapy scared the hell out of me because the side effects are extremely horrible. It changes your overall appearance. But, I resolved that if that needed to be done I would have no problem with it as long as I would have my health back. Undergoing cancer treatment is like taking a gamble. You know of all the side effects yet you are willing to try anything to be in perfect health again. I found out that some women had their breast removed due to the advanced stages of their cancer. The removal of my breast scared me because at that time I was uneducated concerning reconstruction. I was not aware of the cost and if it was covered by my insurance company. Long ago, a mastectomy meant having no breast at all. But now, we are living in modern times where there are options available. Even if there was no reconstruction done on your breast, there are substitutes to fill the void which is a wonderful thing. It takes the shame away from us, without anyone knowing of breast cancer. But, as I mentioned before, whatever it takes to save my life, I would be more than willing to try.

February came and with it the day of my surgery. A snowstorm raged through the night and I wondered whether the hospital would cancel my appointment but they did not. Hospitals do not cancel procedures due to Mother Nature. Doctors and nurses, just like police officers and fire fighters, all find a way to get to their jobs whether rain or snow. A nurse called to confirm my appointment. I was supposed to arrive at the hospital for 7.00am because the surgery was scheduled to be at 9.00am I followed all the instructions after midnight no fluids or foods were to be ingested and I was supposed to bring someone who would be responsible for taking me home after the surgery. That person, of course would be my husband Alton. I got home from work early that evening and packed a small bag. I ate an early dinner and also had a good night's rest. Before going to bed, Alton and I prayed and asked God for favor with the surgery. We prayed that God would guide the doctor's hands and that they would remove whatever needed to be taken out without any complications. After all, they are just humans and can make mistakes but God is the greatest physician of all. I recited Psalm 23, "The Lord Is My Shepherd." I prayed that prayer so fervently that night, telling God that I knew that He would take care of me because He always did. My friends and family who knew about the surgery, they called that night either to pray with me or to give a word of encouragement. After we prayed, I laid in bed thinking about the surgery until I finally fell asleep.

    The morning of the surgery, we left home earlier because we had no idea what the roads would be like from the snow storm the night before. The roads were really messy but we drove with extreme caution. It did not take us long to find a park close to the hospital. My guess was that the workers left their cars home to avoid the agony of the messy roads. We arrived at the hospital much earlier than we anticipated but we did not mind waiting. That way, I could relax and calm my nerves before going into surgery. A few minutes later, my sister in law arrived, I was very happy to see that she was there for me from the beginning, and said that she would be there until it was all over. She was like a mother, never leaving my side. She accompanied me at my appointments when my husband could not be there. I loved her as a mother and I appreciated everything that she did for me in my time of need. Her presence gave me a sense of comfort knowing that she would be with my husband while I was in the operating room. He would not be left alone, h e would have someone to speak with, for comfort and support, rather than knowing him to worry. Besides, they really did get along well as brother and sister. We sat in the waiting area along with a few people,I could not tell who the patients were or who their friends and family members were because everyone looked so serious and afraid. It is sad to see how many people have health issues. Some keep them hidden, while others share their health problems so that they could get the love and support of their family and friends. But whatever it was that brought those people to the hospital, I wished them all well with their procedures and general health.

Finally, the nurse called my name. I took a deep breath and gave my husband a hug thinking that this would have been the last time that I would see him until the surgery was over. However the nurse told us that we would meet each other over at the surgical counseling waiting room where the doctor would talk to us before the procedure. I followed her into the room where she directed my sister in law and me. The nurse took my vital signs and I changed into a hospital gown. A few minutes later, I was escorted by the nurse to the same room where I did my sonogram because they needed to perform another one before the surgery.

After the procedure, we all met in the surgical waiting area which was for patients and their family to relax before going into surgery. While we waited for the doctors, we held hands and prayed for the surgery to be a success. Then the anesthesiologist came in. He explains how he would proceed to place the IV in my arms and how long I would be asleep (Two hours to two -and –a- half). The surgeon came next and explained the procedure to us. I remembered him saying that sometimes procedures like mine could take two to three surgeries but he would try his best so that it would only be one this time. I tried to figure out in my head, How could that be? What he said was confusing but I did not question him any further, I trusted him to do all that needed to be done while I was in surgery. But I guess that's the problem with some of us we don't question the doctors the way we are supposed to so we worry. We agreed with whatever the doctors suggest we don't ask about the side effects or what the medications are supposed to do for us. The nurse came and said that it was time for my surgery, I felt a little nervous knowing that my husband was not going to be with me in the operating room we hugged each other tightly, knowing that the next time we saw each other cancer would be gone and we could continue to enjoy our married life.

I walked into a room that felt like a freezer, I was so cold that I could not grab hold of myself. In the middle of the room there was a long narrow bed surrounded by a lot of equipments. As I looked around I said to myself, "It's going to be all over soon, Nicole, relax and let the doctors do their job". I walked straight to the bed because I knew that is where I was supposed to be. Everyone in the room greeted me with a smile and told me to relax which I was trying to do. I got up on the bed and the nurse covered me with a white sheet from my waist down. She noticed that I was cold so she placed a thick vacuum, hose which was blowing hot air, under the sheets. The anesthesiologist came and did exactly what he said he would, he placed the IV in my left arm which made me sedated. I heard every word that the doctors were saying and sometimes I even felt a slight pinch from what they were doing. It felt as if my skin was being ripped apart with a small knife, but without the pain I kept on saying to myself, "ok, cancer ,you are being ripped apart from a place where you don't belong." You belong in the garbage and that is where they will put you as soon as they are finished with you." I looked straight ahead to the wall I was facing my eyes were closed praying to God for this to be over and done with. Inwardly, I sang all the church songs that I could of remember, so that my mind would be focused on something else other than what was happening to me. As soon as the surgeon finished with the lumpectomy the nurse cleaned me up as best as she could, then I heard her asking another doctor what size bra he thought I would fit into. That sounded so funny at the time a female asking a male about a bra and then I heard him say to her with a giggle, "You should know, You are the female." She went into a room and brought out a white training bra to help me with support until it was time to wear my normal bra again. That would probably be a while. After they put the training bra on me, I was ready to go into the recovery room. As I was being wheeled towards the recovery room, I saw my husband and my sister- in-law

Alton was very excited to see me. He kept smiling and talking about how he called my mother and daughter to let them know that the surgery was a success and that I was doing fine. While I was being cleaned up, the doctor spoke to them about the surgery, stayed in the recovery room for a while. They offered me apple juice and crackers. I was very hungry and my throat felt dry. The doctor who performed the surgery came and told me that everything went well and that I should do a follow up with him in about one week's time. In the meanwhile, I was not allowed to do any heavy lifting and I should avoid bending which would put a strain on my right breast. I was also not allowed to get that area of my body wet in order to avoid any infections until I did a follow up with him. He said that the stitches would dissolve on its own. I was happy to know that the surgery went well so that I could start functioning normally again. Cancer had stolen a lot of my time and energy; I was ready for the next chapter in my life. I stayed in the recovery room for a few more minutes, because I felt sore from the surgery and I was barely able to move my right side. Each time I attempted to get up from the bed I felt like I was being tied down. Something was preventing me from getting out of that position on the bed. I wanted to use the bathroom which was located right in front of me. It was something that I had to do. I had a previous bladder issue from giving birth to my daughter and I had to convince myself that I could go without any difficulties. I did. I was 100% ready to go home. The uncomfortable feeling was still with me because it was normal for anyone to feel that way after surgery. However I was ready to leave the hospital. Alton helped me get dressed. When we were finished he called the nurse and told her that I was ready to be discharged. She handed my husband the discharge form. Attached to it was an instruction sheet which I would have to follow carefully. Next, she gave him a prescription for oxcyclone. A medicine for the pain. Then we left the hospital.

Each time I tried to lift my right arm it restricted me from doing what I wanted to do. The right breast was covered with bandages but part of it was clear so I had a partial view where I could see the swelling. It took me a long time to sponge bathe myself because my right hand was not that workable. I had to take it very slowly and with extra precautions. The training bra started to feel extremely tight. Maybe I should have gotten a size bigger. I eventually switched to a gym bra. It was more relaxing but Alton had to help get it on because lifting my arm was painful. My husband took good care of me during those few days of rest. He prepared meals, did laundry and any other household chores that needed to be done. He made sure that we did not run out of anything. My friends who knew about the surgery called as the days went by, giving all the encouragement that they could. They asked if there was anything they could bring over to the house. I refused the offers of food because my husband was doing a great job in that area and any extras would just go to waste. My mother and daughter called at every spare moment. I felt special. Everyone showed their love towards me. My church family was keeping abreast with my health and they were all praying and believing God for a full recovery for me.

During the day when I was home alone there was nothing much for me to do rather than eat, watch television and read the bible. When I got tired of all three, I would sleep. That was my daily routine. Alton was home from work earlier than usual but he would always call before to ask if he could get me anything special from the store. I thought that was very kind and thoughtful of him. He did a wonderful job when he was home serving me in whatever area he could. I would say that he was my server. When I wanted something from the kitchen, he would kindly get up and get whatever I needed. I missed his presence home with me when he was not in the house. I missed him also being not at home because there was no-one in the house to talk with. He wanted to take time off from working to be home with me but I told him there was no need to do that. I knew that I would be sleeping most of the time. If I think that I wanted him home with me I would definitely let him know. My boss called to find out how I was feeling because I took the time off from work to recover. She knew about my breast cancer diagnosis because she looked at me one day when I was feeling down and knew that something was wrong and I opened up to her. She showed a lot of compassion towards me and I felt happy to know that she was concerned about my health. She said if ever I needed anything or time off for medical appointments, I should let her know. I was mainly concerned about the many doctors' appointments and how it would affect my job, so I was relieved to hear that. As the days went by I started to feel stronger in my body, I was glad that the surgery was over and I was regaining my strength. I started to feel myself again. I was ready to start doing the things I once loved to do. I was happy that cancer cells were no longer a part of me. The next step would be to start the radiation therapy because the doctor had said from the beginning that there was no need for me to have chemotherapy. Once I did the radiation everything would be find. I can move forward with my life and put cancer behind me. I was looking to see the doctor for my follow up, but no one ever told me that after the surgery, I would have to wait a few weeks for the pathology report. Once surgery was over that was it I thought. These were questions that we should have asked during my consultation but we did not because of our lack of knowledge about cancer.

JOY

The morning of my follow up with the doctor I was really anxious to get the stitches out because I wanted the scar to heal the way it was supposed to. I wanted to visit my mother back in Trinidad. I missed her so much. Every day I would think about how she was coping with my father's death. I knew that she was surrounded by friends and family but I still wanted to be present with her in her grief. I missed not being able to attend my father's funeral too. Imagine not being at your father's funeral when you are the only child and he had been a fantastic loving father to me. It hurt so much not being able to say goodbye. But, I had to do what was right for my health at the time. My appointment was at 1.00pm but I got there at around 11.00am. The doctor who performed the surgery had been in an emergency so I saw a different doctor. He asked how I was feeling and looked at my breast and removed the stitches. He said that the scar was healing nicely. The results from the pathology report would not be in another two to three weeks he said. Then he finally said what I have been waiting to hear for the past few weeks "I could visit my mother in Trinidad". Nothing mattered after hearing him speak those words. It was as if he were saying "You've won a million dollars". It was the moment I had been waiting for. It was the best news I had heard since my cancer diagnosis. Somehow, after hearing the doctor tell me that I could go to Trinidad, all other questions which I had planned on asking seemed to vanish right out of my head.

The minute I left the doctor's office I called the travel agency and booked flights for my husband and myself to Trinidad. We were already at the end of one week so I booked for the following week, giving myself some time to grab a few personal items to take with us. As the days went by, I started to feel overwhelmed with joy because I was longing to see my mother we had not tell her as yet that we were planning to visit it was to be a surprise. All I wanted from the time I was diagnosed was to be in my mother's arms where she would nurture me back to reality. It would be a big emotional relief to know that her daughter was coming home to spend some time with her we both needed that. We had both endured the sorrow of death but I had an extra sorrow added to my grief which was my cancer diagnose and my mother still had not been told the truth about my health. I told her eventually that Alton and I was coming on a visit. Within a split second her mood had change over the phone. Her tone of voice was more alive and energetic. She then started to talk and say that she has to clean the room which we will be staying in. She was making preparations already for us and I was happy that she was joyful instead of sad. The trip would do me well, I would be able to take my mind off everything that had happened around me. I wanted to be in a fresher atmosphere, near the beach, away from the cold winter weather in New York. I would make the beach my sanctuary where I would go and be at peace with myself. I also missed eating my mother's home cooked meals. We would have a time of connecting, with my friends whom I have not seen for a while, but after all that fantasizing about what I would do when I got there a rush of sadness came upon me, as I started thinking that my father and my brother would not be there to welcome me home. They were no longer in the land of the living and that brought tears to my eyes. That was not how I imagined going back home to visit but that was how things had turned out. My father died from a stroke, my brother was murdered and there was nothing I could do but adjust myself to the family changes. I consider myself to be a family person. It is in my nature to see a happy family together. No matter whether the situation is good or bad, families should stick by each other.

During the next few days, as I prepared myself for the trip to visit my mother, my mind was completely off cancer which brought a lot of healing to my soul. I wanted to look good for my mother; I kept wondering what to wear and how I should style my hair. My mind and my soul were at rest. I was no longer sore from surgery, I felt good. But, even if it didn't I did not pay it any attention because nothing and no-one was going to come in the midst. A new me had been activated. I was ready to take on the world, ready to live and enjoy the life that God had given to me. I was ready to go to Trinidad and enjoy the company of my mother and my daughter. I loved every minute of the idea. My mind had been transformed from sadness to happiness; cancer no longer had a hold of me I felt like I was in control of my life again. I was winning, or should I say I did win over cancer. Although the doctor did not receive the pathology test to confirm that everything was okay, there was a joy inside of me that no human being could have taken away. I was not going to let anyone steel my joy.

The trip to Trinidad was meant to be a three week vacation for Alton and I. But he was only going to stay for one week. He wanted to give me the space so I could have some alone time with both my mother and my daughter and, he needed to get back to work. We left early in the morning. I felt very comfortable and relaxed on the entire flight. As we drew nearer to our destination, I kept wondering what would be my first response on encountering my mother whom I loved and adored so much. The plane landed and we went through customs like everyone else. At the arrival waiting area I saw my mother. I walked straight to her and then we embraced each other. She was very happy, that was the happiest I have ever seen her and it felt good. My husband interrupted us with a hello and also hugged her. It felt wonderful to be home again in my country where I was born.

Everything looked so different after being away from home for such a long time. My daughter was at the house waiting for us. It has been a year since we last saw each other. She came to the United States the year before where she stayed with Alton and I for a while. She was also very excited to have us both home. Our trip was a success because we both went to places and did things that we never thought we would have done. It was Alton's first visit to the Caribbean and he was enjoying every moment of it.

One day, I decided to show my mother the scar on my breast. She asked again as she did before if it was cancerous and off course I said no. I hated lying to my mother, but at the same time I was not ready to put her in that kind of mood. If she knew that it was cancer she would be devastated. One of the most memorable times I had, was when my mother and I would just sit and talk about my father. She would tell me hilarious things and I would burst into laughter. Then I would repeat the excitement by telling her about the times he would call me in the United States with a childish problem which I thought at the time was funny. She would laugh hysterically. It was good to see my mother laughing after all the sorrow and pain that she had been through. We never talked much about what happened to my brother. He was murdered and we both never healed thoroughly from his loss. Talking about him might change the atmosphere which I did not want to happen. I enjoyed being home with my family. It gave me a sense of comfort and relaxation because I was able to spent time with my mother, daughter and husband at the same time. At times we would all go out together. Just before our visit to Trinidad was coming to an end my mother had a surprise party for us. All of the neighbors were invited along with some friends whom I had not seen for a long time. The party was for our anniversary because it was the first one since our marriage. There were lots of food and drinks for everyone. I enjoyed the company of my friends Alton spend his evening chatting with a few of the men telling them all about America. The night ended and we were about to face another day with more attractions and excitements.

BACK TO REALITY

The appointment to see the doctor was scheduled for the week I came back to the states. My vacation was coming to an end and I felt sadness on the inside of me. I wished that I could have extended my stay but I could not because of my doctor's appointment. I hated to leave my mother so soon but there was nothing I could have done to change that. I enjoyed spending every day with her and my daughter. We spent such memorable times together. It seemed like we bonded all over again. I never spent such quality time with them before; we said our sad goodbyes at the airport. Alton only stayed in Trinidad for one week and I spent three. We had never been away from each other for such a long time since we got married so I was anxious to be back in New York.

I was happy to see him at JFK Airport. I called my mother as soon as I got to the house to let her know that I was home safely. As the days drew closer to my doctor's appointment, I tried to keep my mind only on good memories of my trip, nothing else. I had such a wonderful time I wish that it had not ended. It was a long time since I went to the beach. The next morning, Alton and I went to the appointment to get the results from the pathology test, as we waited for my name to be called, I tried to keep as focused as possible. Finally, they called Nicole Lineszy we went into the office sat down face to face with the doctor then out came the words from his mouth: "Your pathology test came back positive you will need to have a second surgery." It was not what we wanted to hear after coming from a beautiful vacation where we placed cancer and everything behind us hoping that my life would move forward. It seemed as if I was reliving the torment which once haunted and took control of me, cancer was still a part of me it was not completely gone like I wanted it to be it was still in my life without permission. Now I had to go through the agony and the discomfort of another surgery, how could that be? What went wrong? It was not fair for me to be going under another surgery so soon. Why was life treating me this way? I was back in depression mode once more. It seemed like the disease had no intentions of finding its way out, a few weeks ago I felt like I was reliving my life. Now, it was as if I was diagnosed all over again I wondered if this would ever end.

The doctor said before that some patients do need a second surgery but I doubted it would be me, I did not ask why at that particular time, my mind had been transformed again this time from happiness to sadness. My body was like a switch being turned on and off to different moods it worked well because I was reacting to it perfectly, it was as if my life had been set back. The things that I had planned for my husband and I were about to be delayed everything around me was on hold it was as if the pause button had been pushed. I was not in remission I didn't even start cancer treatment, however I was given the sad news again about my health; the cancer was not out completely. The doctor explained that sometimes things like that happen since my cancer was called a DCIS, he used an orange as a metaphor to explain what was happening inside my breast. He went on to say that if you have an orange and part of it is spoiled; you cut out the spoiled part, but the area around it may still be infected. To get the infections all out you would have to cut around the orange again until you get all of the infected part out. That was what he needed to do with my breast. He needed to go in again and clean around where the tumor was, but he said that sometimes things like that happens and that everything would be fine once he cleaned out the infected area. I was not happy to hear all that since I just came out of surgery. Hearing that news seemed like a nightmare to me.

The idea of cutting me open again seemed senseless. I asked myself why all of that was not done the first time since he was the doctor and he knew of that possibility. He could have prevented a second surgery by doing all the necessary steps. It was not fair for me or for my family to go through that again. It seemed as if we were going backwards instead of forwards. This was my life. I was a human being, not something to be experimented on. I started to think that maybe there was money involved. The doctor would be paid each time I went into surgery. Within a month's time I was scheduled for a second surgery

My body was not completely healed from the first but here I was making plans with the doctor for a second surgery. I was told just as the first time, about the pretesting and what needed to be done. He handed me my prescription slip for the surgery, then my husband and I left the office. I was not happy at all I kept quiet, I did not feel like talking on our way home. My husband kept asking if I was alright and I nodded my head each time he asked. We were both very unhappy with the idea of having to undergo surgery again. We still did not figure out why it was not done the first time. When we got to the house I phoned a few of my friends and told them what was happening. They all said the same thing that I had said which was, why did they not do all of this the first time? What if they're not telling me everything?

One o f my friends from church had given me a book by Susan Summers in which she mentioned how she was wrongfully diagnosed with full blown body cancer. I kept asking myself. What if it is not Cancer and it was just a cyst? Am I being experimented on? There was no one in my family who had ever had a cancer before, I doubted my doctors for a moment but then again, I did not have a medical degree so I trusted them since I did not know better.

I went to a different doctor to get a second opinion about the pathology test and he confirmed I really did have breast cancer after all. But why all the different surgeries? Although I was hearing all the different reports, I was not ready to give up on life or my family. I was willing and ready to put up a fight so that I could live, but just not live, live to fulfill my destiny and my purpose which God has created me to do.

Surgery number two was scheduled for the week before Easter. I did the pretest, went through all the explaining did all the blood work, including the EKG, I was ready to get it all over with. Nothing was new to me now. I was rebuilding my physical strength after the first surgery. Now, some of it was going to be taken away from me again. The morning of the surgery I arrived at the hospital. Again it was an early morning surgery. I checked myself into the Ambulatory department. I prayed and asked God again for a successful second surgery, without having to go back for a third. I wanted this to be the end of it all. No more surgical procedures. It still seemed like a mistake to me but could not be proven. The only thing which changed is that I did not need to have a sonogram. The nurse gave me a pill which she said would prevent any nauseous feelings from the anesthesia after surgery. We met with the doctors in the patients operating waiting room. First the anesthetist came in and asked a lot of personal questions for which we needed privacy away from the other two companions who came with us. We left, the surgeon came. He too explained what his procedure was then he left. As we waited for the nurse to come and take me to the operating room I said to myself, God please let there be no more surgery after this one. I wanted the doctors to do their best while I was under their care. I wanted them to remove all of the unwanted cells which did not belong with the good cells. A few minutes after, the nurse came in to take me into the theater but before leaving with her, my husband and I hugged each other. It was the kind of hug he gave when he wanted to give assurance of his love. After all the embracing, I departed from my husband and left with the nurse down the aisle towards the surgical theater.

The operating room was cold as usual. The nurse placed the hose with the hot air under the sheets so that I could be warm. The anesthesiologist injected me. I fell asleep while I was trying to count. It's as if you know that you will be falling to asleep in no time yet you try to fight the feeling and you end up on the losing side.

I awoke to the sound of the doctor calling my name. I looked up, saw the clock on the wall, and said to myself "it must have been a long one." The doctor said that the procedure was over and I would be placed in the recovery room until I felt well enough to leave. The nurse already placed a training bra on me which I hoped was the right size this time, because I did forget to tell her what size fit me best. I was placed in the recovery room where there were other patients recovering from surgery.

Back To Reality

It was already late in the afternoon. As soon as I was settled in the recovery room, my friend from church and Alton's sister left saying that they loved me and they would call later on to check on me. I remembered that suddenly I started to feel dizzy, I told the nurse and she checked my blood pressure which was higher than a normal reading. She asked if I normally have high blood pressure, I told her sometimes. But this was way too high. She said that I could get a stroke if something was not done immediately. All I could remember was the bottom number being 129. She gave me a pill but it did not work that well because my blood pressure was still very high. I was hungry and thirsty at the same time because it was late in the afternoon and I had nothing to eat since the night before. I begged for something to eat for a long time. Then the nurse finally brought in a light snack. I ate it all within seconds because I was hungry. Alton and I talked for a little bit then he left to go get himself something to eat as well. When he left, I felt the urge to pass urine, so I told the nurse that I needed a bedpan. She bought it for me but for some reason I could not urinate and it was starting to create great pain in my lower abdomen. I called the nurse again and told her what was happening but she kept telling me to try. Then she walked away and attended to someone else. I started to panic since I contracted bladder problems after giving birth to my daughter. I spoke to a different nurse who was attending to someone else and told her that I was in an urgent need to go to the bathroom because the bed pan was not working for me. I thought maybe if I could go sit on the commode it would be much better for me. She told me that in a few minutes she would take me to the bathroom. I needed her to help me because I was not strong enough to go on my own. I felt weak and the bag with the drip needed to be assembled to the pole so that I would be able to take it with me. I called her again telling her that the urge was right there and I felt like I wanted to urinate on myself. She finally came and helped me to the bathroom, but left after I got in so that I could have my privacy. After using the bathroom, I felt a tremendous dizziness and nauseous feeling came upon me. My body could not carry my weight anymore. My strength had been taken away from me. It was a feeling I had never experienced before. Until then I didn't know what was happening to me , I called the nurse for help. I begged her to please come quickly. I was about to hit the floor, I tried to brace myself from falling by leaning onto the wall. At that time beads of sweat were rolling down my face, still there was no nurse to help me in my agony and take me back to the bed where I belonged. There were nurses sitting at the front desk but neither of them offered to help instead they kept saying that my nurse will be right with me as soon as she finish with the other patient. It's unbelievable how people can be treated in the hospital. I was completely ignored by the nurses and I started to feel emotionally hurt as well. At this time I was very dissatisfied with the service that I was getting from this hospital. My energy was drained. I could not do or say anything. I just wanted the horrible feeling to go away.

My husband walked into the recovery room and saw an expression on my face that he had never seen before. He knew right away that something was not right so he took me to the bed. As soon as I hit the bed, I started vomiting all over myself. I felt a relief come over me when it was over but I was still having the strange feeling with what was happening in my bladder. Why was it not acting the way it was supposed to? My husband called the nurse and told her what I had done to myself. She had given herself double work then because she had not responded to my call before. The sheets on the bed needed to be changed along with the clothes that I was wearing. She came and gave me a lot of ice to suck on to make me feel better.

The doctor was paged because my blood pressure was still high. He was told what was happening so he decided to keep me overnight. Oh boy, here it comes again, that urging sensation along with the pain in my abdomen. I tried to use the bed pan which the nurse had kept under me. However I was only able to pass maybe one teaspoon of urine from my body. Not good. I could tell that something was wrong because that was not how my body was supposed to react. Every ten minutes I was getting the urge to urinate without any progress passing, fear took over me. What had they done to me in the operating room? I started to get flashbacks after I had my daughter and the bladder problem was created. While giving birth, I had a ruptured bladder and was rushed into surgery. This was the same feeling I had back then.

I tried to explain to the nurse that I had a bladder problem a few years earlier but she paid me no attention. I called my mother as soon as she left and told her what was happening although she was not present with me; she was the only one that understood the distress I was in. She was at my side a few years back when the problem started and she told me to drink plenty of water or suck lots of ice. All these memories kept invading my mind. I did not want a repeat of what had happened then because that was a nightmare that I will never forget as long as I live. My husband called the nurse to my side. I explained to her a second time the situation concerning my bladder history, along with the pain and discomfort that I was having. This time with tears in my eyes. She finally decided to put a catheter in me. The minute the tube entered my bladder the urine started to flow and I felt relief. The urine bag was full in such a short space of time that the nurse decided to leave the catheter in for a while. At that moment nothing mattered to me as long as the urine was coming out and not backing up.

The nurse said that as soon as there was an available bed I would be taken to a room upstairs because my blood pressure was still high and needed to be controlled. It took a while for them to find a bed up stairs, but as soon as they did I was placed in a room all by myself. I was tired after having a busy and troublesome day so it did not take me long to fall asleep. But when I did, I was awakened in the middle of the night by a male nurse wanting to draw blood from me and also to monitor my blood pressure. I was given blood pressure medication again; my blood pressure was still high. Minutes later, I was asleep. I must have slept right through the night because the sound of a good morning coming from two Jamaican nurses whom I had met the night before, woke me. They provided me with toiletries to get cleaned up, when they left the room, I gave myself a sponge bath on the bed. I brushed my teeth and combed my hair so that I would be clean when the doctor came. Breakfast was served. I was hungry so I ate what was brought to me which was very fulfilling. My sister in law came during visiting hours. We talked for a few minutes then she left. The doctor came a couple of hours after to check on my progress from the high blood pressure the day before. He said that It was not necessary for me to stay over after the surgery. However because of the high blood pressure, they had no other choice than to admit me for an overnight stay. He said the surgery was a success and I should not worry about having a third one. He told me that, the reason why I had bladder problems was due to the long period of time I had stayed in the operating room under the anesthesia .The surgery took much longer than they had anticipated. He signed the release form to send me home and said I should visit him in a week for a follow up then he left.

    I called my husband to let him know that I was being discharged from the hospital so that he could come and take me home. That was the first time after giving birth to my daughter that I was admitted into a hospital but I was very comfortable and satisfied with the room that they gave to me. I almost did not want to leave despite the confusion that I had experienced the day before. While I waited for my husband, I called my friends to let them know that everything was fine and that I was being released from the hospital. My right breast felt stiff. It felt as if I was carrying a heavy load on my chest. When Alton came, he assisted me in getting dressed because it was very difficult to move my right arm without help. We waited for the prescription from the doctor which took a while. He prescribed anti-cyclone again for me which was becoming my favorite because it worked well when I had the first surgery. We left the hospital room and headed to the car. There was pulling in my chest from the surgery, so I could not walk at the speed which I normally did and also there was a lot of snow on the ground so I had to be very careful. Alton held my hand while I tried to sit in the car. I had to remind him to try and avoid any bumps or pot holes in the roads while driving. We stopped by the pharmacy to fill the prescriptions, and then we got some vegetable soup.

    It was good to be home; I ate, took my medications and went to lie in my bed. A few minutes after, I fell asleep and awoke late afternoon. Due to the medications I could not keep myself awake, I ate and fell right back to sleep I have to admit that it felt good. My body and my mind needed the relaxation and besides the doctor said resting would be part of my healing process. Later in the afternoon I received a lot of phone calls, everyone wanted to know how I was progressing.

Back To Reality

The next morning when I awoke, the stiffness on my right side was extremely unbearable I felt that I could not pull myself out from bed. After a few minutes of trying I got up with my left hand supporting my right breast which was twice its usual size. The pain was even more severe than the day before I felt that I should take one of the pain killers which was oxycodone,I was not allowed to take a shower until my follow up with the doctor. Wetting the surgical area would only create problems and cause infection. I undressed myself slowly with one hand. I removed the support bra which was put on after the surgery. I looked down at my breast which were so swollen that it looked two times the size it was before, even covered in bandages. After giving myself a sponge bath, I had breakfast then took my medications. I knew right away that I would fall asleep but that did not bother me due to the intense pain I was having. Drowsiness took over my body in a short space of time. I could barely keep my eyes open. I felt as if I was on drugs. My head kept falling from side to side. Then I fell asleep. Sleeping on my back was getting to be a nuisance to me. It was the only body position I could lay on for the time being until my body felt normal again. When I was awake I indulged myself in the pain killers. It was the best thing that was happening to me. They were my best friends when I was in discomfort. Alton reminded me that I should not get too addicted because it has been said on the news on several occasions that people do get addicted to ox cyclone and abuse the pill. I knew to myself that I was beginning to be one of the abusers but the pill made me feel good by taking away the pain and discomfort. When in pain, a person would do and take whatever there is for ease, at that moment in my life I was doing whatever I had to in order to ease the physical pain, I felt that I could not go through the healing process.

As the days went by, I continued taking oxycodone. I needed to stop doing that to myself but I could not, I took the pill even when I had no pain and I wanted to sleep. This is the part of my journey no-one knew about. Not even my husband. In order to stop taking the pills I hid them far out of my sight because I thought If I could see them every time I walked by I would have the urge for one. I finally quit taking the medication, I no longer needed them because the pain had subsided and I was sleeping on my own without its help.

I was taking oxycodone for the wrong reasons but thanks to God for delivering me from the medication and my stupidity.

I went back to the doctor's office for my follow up along with my husband. I was ready to take the bandages off and also very anxious to get cancer behind me. The nurse called my name and we both went in ready to get it all over and done with. The doctor's assistant came in removed the dressing and said that everything looked fine, however the breast was still swollen from surgery. The stitches looked perfect. She removed as many of them as possible and said that the rest will dissolve by themselves. She said the doctor who performed the surgery would be in shortly to speak to us. We sat there for almost an hour thinking that he was busy with another patient and would come as soon as he is was free. However he never came in, we were sitting there when a doctor came in and asked if we were waiting to be seen by a doctor. We told her the name of the doctor whom we were waiting to see but to our surprise, he was gone for the day. I was bewildered by the whole scenario. I did not understand the confusion but that was what happened. He left the office without seeing us. His assistant told us that she was very sorry for what had happened. She looked at the pathology results on the computer and said that all the results were fine and that she would schedule me for an appointment to see the radiologist. There was no need for me to have chemotherapy only the radiation treatment. But the radiologist would have to tell me himself how much treatment I would need. The healing process required more time so they scheduled my appointment for radiation treatment in one month. Not having chemotherapy was very satisfying to me because of what I learned about the side effects. I was scared to put my body through that, but if I had to I most definitely would to save my life.

As I waited for my appointment to see the radiologist, I tried to eat as healthy as possible; I took vitamins on a daily basis and ate in order to gain enough strength to withstand the treatment. I continued to do my research on breast cancer radiation therapy. I wanted to educate myself and to know exactly what I was dealing with; I learned that the longevity on the treatment depends on your diagnoses. I spoke to many people whom I knew underwent the treatment about what it felt like during and after the procedure. I was determined to find the answers to the questions. I learned about the terrible disease which had taken so many lives in the past and still do today. Cancer does not have an age limit neither does it discriminates. It does not come your way by how much money you have or whether you are good or bad it just attacks you. It comes to invade your body and to take you out. It's one of our biggest enemies. It is a disease in our society. It has no mercy on which it leeches on, we the victims who have to fight for our lives. We cannot give up without a fight.

The minute Cancer sees that we are giving up it says "I got you" and things begin to get worse. Having a lot of support from family and friends gave me the energy and also the encouragement to move and to be strong. One day I laid in bed with the curtains drawn aside to have a clear view of the sky. As I looked up, I just kept wondering what is the meaning of all this. Why was I facing this difficulty with cancer? I just wanted it to all go away. Then I told myself, regardless of what comes my way, I will still trust God. One night I dreamt that there was an angel telling me that God reigns and I kept saying it over and over. Alton must have heard because the next thing I remembered was that he was woke me up because he thought that I was having a nightmare. I felt joy and peace in my spirit because I knew that God was with me in the midst of it all and that everything would be alright. My breast was starting to get smaller due to the surgeries that had taken place. Every time the doctors performed surgery on the breast, they would be removing the bad tissue cells which made up a portion of my breast. Because of that, the breast has been shrinking to a smaller size. I started to avoid looking at myself in the mirror because I was displeased with the fact that one breast was smaller than the other. When I went out in public places I would wonder if anyone noticed the difference. The minute someone stared at me I said "Yes they know "and it bothered me. I even tried wearing padded bras but that did not do much help. The radiation therapy was going to shrink my breast even more because that was part of the side effect. What will I be left with I wondered.

The evening of my appointment with the radiologist I was very nervous because I did not know what to expect once I got there. I went in, gave my name to the receptionist, and waited for someone to call my name. A few minutes later I was called in. The nurse introduced herself then she asked questions when was my last surgery. I told her and she said "good." Then I was definitely ready to start my treatment. She explained to me that today was my first day and they would be doing a lot of x-ray. She made the markings on my breast with a permanent marker. This is so the machine would pin point exactly where I needed the radiation. She also said that it would be a five week treatment, which meant that for five weeks I would have to come to the hospital for the treatment and I should have someone with me in case I felt nauseous. The schedules were very flexible I choose a time that was convenient to me. She seemed very nice. I felt comfortable with her. She said that she would be right back because she needed to check my pathology report on the computer and also the doctor, who was the radiologist, would talk to me before the procedure begins.

Within a few minutes, the doctor was in with a folder in his hand. He looked at both of us, and asked which doctor had referred me to start the radiation therapy. I told him what had happened that day and the doctor's assistant had looked at the report, said that the pathology test was negative and that I could start the treatment. But he said sorry, there was no way that he could start the radiation therapy because the report showed that there were still cancer cells which needed to be taken out and that I would need to have a mastectomy done. He said that was the only way to get all of the cancer cells out before I started the treatment.

Tears came to my eyes right away. I could not believe what I was hearing. He must have misunderstood the report. My husband told him at the last appointment I had, the doctor said I was fine and ready for the radiation therapy. He said no, there must be a mistake by whoever sent me to him. He could not understand why they sent me for radiation when the pathology test was still reading positive. He said that he would not give me any treatment because it would do me no good; the only solution was for me to have a mastectomy. The word seemed so easy for him to say. He said it with no remorse or sympathy. Then he finally said there is always reconstruction to consider.

By that time I was speechless, Alton was doing all the talking. I was numb. He told the doctor that there was no way that I would do a mastectomy without having a second opinion. My husband held my hand and we left the hospital. Tears were streaming down my face I could not believe what my ears just heard. Did he just say the word mastectomy? I called my cousin while I waited for Alton to come from using the bathroom. I was in tears with her on the phone. At the same time I explained to her that the doctor just told me that I would have to go through another surgery, she was also very puzzled by his words and said we should get another opinion. She said it seemed as if they were using me as a guinea pig to experiment on.

I cried all the way home. I did not even feel like talking anymore to anyone although Alton kept saying; we will not listen to them we will go somewhere else to get a second opinion. Every time I thought about what the doctor said to me my heart got filled with sadness, I felt as if the doctors was keeping something from me. One doctor said everything was fine, the other something different I felt confused, not knowing what to do. Was my life slipping away? Was I going to die because of breast cancer? I felt so down it seemed like I had been diagnosed with cancer all over again. My life started to flash right in front of me. My whole mindset changed. Immediately I started to think all the negative thoughts.

I felt that there was no life inside of me. I felt empty, I felt lifeless. Nothing made sense. I felt betrayed by my surgeon. Maybe he saw the report the day I was supposed to see him in the office and maybe he knew that there would be a need for a third surgery and could not face telling me that news. I was very confused, troubled and angry about the situation. Why was I having all of these surgeries over and over again? It's like I had breast cancer diagnosis three times. They did not say that in words to me but that was exactly how I felt each time they mentioned surgery to me. Something was not right with this doctor. Why all the surgeries?

I could not believe that all of this was happening. I already made up in my mind that I was going to start the radiation process today and put all of the cancer behind me, so that I could continue to live a happy life with my husband. I felt as if I was banned from being happy. I just wanted to enjoy my life like any other married woman. That was all I wanted to do. Instead I was sad about cancer. That night; we phoned all of our relatives, including the church family (Pastor) to inform them of what was happening. They could not believe the confusion that had happened. Everyone said the same words to me "Get a second opinion." My whole mindset had suddenly changed. I was now in depression mode again because I was very uncertain about my health. I did not know who to believe. Whether I was cancer free or not. My emotions for the past few months were not stable. I was depressed too many times which was not good for my mental health. Was I suppose to have the radiation therapy or was I to have a mastectomy? Both answers remained unclear to me because one doctor was saying that I was ready for treatment the other said no. I was in the middle of a tug-of war but this was not a game, this was my life.

I needed help finding a doctor to get a second opinion. I did not know of any that dealt with that area at the time. The burden was more than I could handle. The weight was too much for me alone to bear. How can a human being go through so much difficulty with a sickness? Was I strong enough to fight my cancer ordeal or was I just going to let it win? I had no idea. That was how confused I became. I wanted comfort, I wanted peace, I wanted all of this mess to go away, Nicole Lineszy, wanted her health back. I started to think of my mother and my daughter. How was I going to explain to my mother about a third surgery after I had already told her the first and the second time that it was just a cyst? I could not have gone under anesthesia without telling my mother because God forbid something happened, I would not have wanted my husband to be blamed. But now she would know that something was wrong. Then what would my daughter think? Would she be scared? Finally I picked up the phone, dialed my daughter's number and told her what was happening. She was very supportive of me I did not talk to my mother that night because I was not ready to tell her another lie. Would she ever forgive me for not telling her the truth? My feelings were being hurt over and over again, I felt betrayed by my own body.

I was ashamed of myself because there was nothing I could have done to prevent what was happening; it was beyond any human control. I could not get over the feeling inside of me. Was it going to go away? How long would I be this way? There were no words that could comfort me at that time. My husband tried but he had no luck. How could anyone know the way that I was feeling? They were not diagnosed with cancer, so they had no idea what I was dealing with. How I wished that it was all a nightmare. But every time I looked in the mirror there was my reminder, every time I turned around it was all in my head. I wanted to be set free from all agony and emotional pain.

My life was beginning to feel like an avalanche. Everything around me was falling down. It was like a broken puzzle where the pieces needed to be put back together again. I needed help and I needed it fast. But, where was I going to start to look for that help? Later that night, after feeling a little better, I remembered watching the television many times and seeing the commercial from the cancer society of America where people talked about being healed from treatment that was best for them. I was determined to get some answers, why I needed to have a third surgery. I did a search on the computer for the number and guess what. There it was: the 1-800 numbers for the Cancer Society of America which was in Philadelphia. I dialed the number with excitement; spoke with the operator explaining to her my condition. She was very attentive to what I had to say but she suggested that since I lived in New York. I should visit a hospital back there because the journey to go back and forth would be a lot for me. She said that there were a few good hospitals in my area such as NYU Cancer Center, Stone Memorial Kettering and also New York Presbyterian Hospital. She wished me best of luck in my health then we said our goodnight.

As soon as I came off the phone I dialed the NYU Cancer Center but because it was late at night I got a recording. I left my name and telephone number. Next, I dialed the Stone Memorial Kettering Hospital. I heard about this hospital before and that cancer treatments are their specialty. I spoke to an operator and told her what was happening with me. She transferred me to the nursing department. However they said that they could only give me a second opinion due to the fact that I was already seen by another hospital. I felt relief to know that I was getting somewhere; I did not call New York Presbyterian because I figured that I would wait on NYU to hear what they had to say. I went to bed feeling satisfied with what I had achieved earlier.

I gave God thanks the next morning as soon as I woke up from my sleep. I thanked him that despite all that I was facing, I was still alive and that it was another day for me to win the battle. It was the weekend so there was nothing much that I could of done but to wait for Monday morning and the response from the hospital. The weekend seemed to be moving slower than normal; the anxiety in me began to rise again. I was desperate for answers. There was a friend of the family who lived in Pennsylvania, and was once diagnosed with breast cancer many years ago. I called her to get information about her doctor and the care she received. We were highly recommended by her to the doctor but when I thought about it, I told my husband that it would not work for us. There was no way I could go to Pennsylvania for a surgery and have treatment all the way up there every day. It made no sense at all. The help that I was searching for had to be close to home. We decided to wait until Monday to hear what the NYU Cancer Centerhad to offer.

Monday morning was finally here I did not wait for them to call, I made the call. I told them what was happening and that I would appreciate if they would let me come in for a second opinion. The receptionist agreed and made an appointment for the following week because the doctor was away on vacation. I agreed since I had no choice or did not know where to turn to. I waited one week to see the doctor. That waiting period felt like forever. I felt like I needed to talk to women who had gone through what I was now facing. I joined the Susan Komen Support Group which was on Face book. It was helpful because I got a lot of encouragement from the women who had the same problem that I was facing. I was also recommended by a friend to join the Basia Survivor Group which is for Caribbean women with Breast cancer. The director e-mailed me saying how sorry she was to hear of my diagnosis and that they would keep a close contact with me. A few days later, a survivor from the group called with words of encouragement, telling me not to worry about the diagnosis everything would be just fine. She encouraged me by letting me know that she had a mastectomy and that it was nothing to worry about. She even joked that I should think about it like having newer firmer breasts. Even if the NYU said that I needed to have a mastectomy, I would rather do it with them. Not the previous hospital, they were not allowed to touch me again. I would never trust them with my life ever again.

During the wait, I researched to get as much information as I could about mastectomy and reconstruction. I learned that the two surgeries can be performed in one day and it is not a shameful thing if a woman was to have her breast removed for an implant. There are two types of reconstruction surgeries, one where the doctor uses silicone and the other where body fat or tissue is used to fill the empty space. I tried not to worry during my wait but that was very difficult. I did not know for sure what was happening to me, whether my breast would be taken out or not. Could I still look at myself in the mirror and consider myself beautiful? Should I be labeled or was I to be label as the woman with one breast or the woman with the artificial breast? If I were to lose my breast, would I want people to know, or would I keep it a secret for the rest of my life? These were the questions I kept asking myself I would probably be embarrassed to even let my husband look at me. Would he still be attracted to a one sided woman? He said on several occasions that it did not matter to him if I was one sided or did not have any breast at all because he did not marry me for my breasts, but for who I am, he saw a good woman in me. The very first time he laid eyes on me he knew that I was different from any other. I tried to bring myself to terms with the possibility but I somehow could not. There must be a way out of this; I wanted a miracle from God. Sometimes, I just sit or lay on my bed hoping for the phone to ring and the doctor telling me that it was all a mistake. I didn't have breast Cancer. What a celebration that would be. But, that was just all in my head. I have seen things like that happen in the movies but this were my life and it was all real; there were no actors.

I recalled my life before the diagnosis and how happy I was with no sickness to worry about. It seemed as if my whole world had been turned upside down. My life was like a tornado spinning in circles with no way out and there was nothing I could do to stop it. I just had to try and fight with all of my strength, power and most of all my faith. Monday would soon be here and there would be good news. I had to believe that this too could be fixed because that was what the Almighty God does, He fixes the problem whether big or small. I had to keep my faith pumping to know that my life was not over because of cancer. I have seen the breast cancer walk yearly and everyone whether old or young, fought the disease. Who was I to quit on my life knowing that my assignment in this world was not completed? I was feeling a lot of mixed emotions. Sometimes my husband would say to me you said you are a Christian. Where is your faith? But I was only human responding to my feelings. It does not matter who you are or your religious belief, when you're being diagnosed with cancer it's very hard to not worry about the consequence. It takes a lot of faith to keep a positive attitude.

It was Monday morning, the beginning of May, I was very anxious to go to the NYC Cancer Center to hear what the doctors had to say. My husband and I took the train into Manhattan because we did not know if there would be a parking garage near the hospital. We did not have any difficulties in finding the location because it was right around the corner from Lexington Avenue. Something magical happened. As I walked through the sliding doors at the hospital I immediately felt a sign of relief. Everyone looked so professional in what they were doing. That was the kind of place you would most definitely want to go to when you have cancer. They specialized in all types of cancer and from what I have learned, they were good at it. Out front of the cancer center were a few guys dressed in black pants and white shirt. They were the chauffeurs for the valet parking for the patients who drove to have radiation treatment. All you had to do was pull up out front with your vehicle and the guys would take the car and park it at the hospital garage until your treatment was over. I walked to the front desk at the security guards. I told the gentleman my name. He looked it up on the computer then escorted me to the room behind him where I registered. It took about ten minutes for the clerk to register my name into the computer. When she was all done, she directed me to the elevators which would take me to the fourth floor where I met with the oncologist. My experience with everyone I encountered so far was wonderful. They all seemed so professional. It was as if they were programmed to be nice with everyone that came to the center. We took the elevator up to the fourth floor as we were told to do. There was another receptionist at the nurses' station where I again gave my name along with the folder which was given to me from the receptionist down stairs; we were told to have a seat. The doctor would be with us shortly. There was a computer that we could have made use of if we wanted to, but being on the computer at that time was not in my plans. All I wanted at that point was to hear what the doctor had to say. We both had something cold to drink with a few Graham crackers while we waited to be seen by the doctor.

I sat and looked around at the faces that I saw whom I believed had cancer like myself and were waiting to see the doctor. But all I saw in those faces were sadness and fear. Everyone looked much older than I was, so I felt sympathy for myself seeing that I was the youngest among them all. There was not a lot of talking in the waiting area because of the mood that everyone was in. The only voices we heard came from the nurse calling my name to see the doctor. I tried to study each of their faces without staring directly into their faces. I was interested to know and wished that I could have read some of their minds to know what they were thinking but I was interrupted by my husband.

The nurse called Nicole Lineszy. We both went in. The nurse took my vital signs blood pressure was a little high, which was no surprise to me because of the torment that I had been going through for the past few months. I tried on many occasions to calm myself, but it was no use. I changed into the hospital gown while I waited for the doctor. Next there was a knock on the door and a hello from a doctor. She introduced herself and told me how beautiful I looked. I smiled with a thank you because I tried to look as cute as always for my appointments. After all the compliments she asked "What brought you here today?" I explained everything to her step by step without leaving anything out. As I spoke she took notes and asked questions, at the same time making sure that she had everything correctly. She also asked who referred me to the Cancer Center. I told her, and she was very pleased to hear. She looked at the reports that I brought with me which were my own personal records from the surgeries before. She left the room stating that she would be right back. She needed to show the reports to another doctor. As she left the room my heart was beating twice its normal rare. I felt like I was about to explode. I looked at my husband and he looked at me without either one of us saying a word to each other. Within a few minutes the doctor was back. She said she had to go over the report with another doctor. She said that the Cancer was DCIS and in most cases the breast would have to be taken out. She also explained in full details that leaving the breast may cause a recurrence due to the fact that I was very young. She explained the odds with a younger person versus an older one. I understood the point clearly. She said that it was important for her to have the pathology from the two surgeries that I underwent which meant that I would have to go to the hospital to get the report. But first, I would have to sign a consent release form. It took her a long time to explain the situation to us because she made sure that we understood what was happening. I felt really relaxed with her, although it was not what I had expected to hear. I thought that coming there would end all of my problems pertaining to Cancer I felt comfortable. She asked if I wanted to switch from the hospital that I was going before and my response was yes because I was uncomfortable going back there for medical reasons. She suggested that I see the radiology doctors in the basement to hear their opinion of whether the treatment would work for me or not. My visit to the oncologist would be in a month. That way, she would have all the necessary reports to look at. She assured me that I should not worry, I was in good care. She shook both of our hands and said goodbye. Before leaving the Cancer Center that afternoon, I stopped at the radiation department to make an appointment to see the doctor which the oncologist recommended. The next available date was in two weeks because that is when the doctor would be back from her vacation. There always seemed to be a waiting period no matter how hard I tried.

As we walked to the elevator, my husband asked if I was I satisfied with the doctor and I told him "Yes" the doctor seemed to know perfectly what she was talking about. Unlike the other hospital she took the time to explain everything to us about the cancer. When we got back to Brooklyn, I went to the hospital to sign the form for my medical records to be released and sent to the NYU Cancer Center but they said that it would take ten working days. I left the medical records department with confidence and relief to know that I was getting somewhere.

That night, my husband and I discussed our visit with NYU Cancer Center with the in-laws, letting them know what was taking place and that we were highly satisfied with the doctor and what she had to say.

I was ready then and willing to do whatever was right for my life. Alton was very pleased with the decisions that I made pertaining to my health. He was glad to know that I was ready to trust the doctors at NYU Cancer Center because of my satisfaction with their overall performance. Over the next days I did a lot of praying, trusting and believing in God to bring me through this torment of cancer. That is what Cancer was doing to me, tormenting my life daily from one surgery into another. I tried to do other things to keep my mind clear. The doctor suggested that I take long walks in the park because it was the spring season and everything was blooming and beautiful, the outside atmosphere would do me good. I followed her advice. I loved treating myself at the ice cream parlor. I tried to make it there almost every Sunday after church. I was trying to take in a lot of calories because I was told that I should because one of the side effects of radiation therapy is losing weight. Gaining now, I would not have to worry about my outer appearance so much. I started exercising every morning which I was also told would improve my heath and keep my immune system healthy. I got up at six every morning and walk around the park. The doctor said that I was not active enough in my life and the walking would boost my energy. Changing my diet was one of the things I had changed drastically. I was eating more fish than chicken, brown rice instead of white rice with more greens on my plate. I started feeling like a child being forced to eat their vegetables because I was never the kind of person to have greens on my plate. Spinach, I didn't like, collard greens no-way forget it. But now I don't complain, I just buy, cook, eat and enjoy whatever vegetables are on my plate. Juicing, is what I started doing with fruits and vegetables. There is a lot of cancer fighting foods on the market which some of us don't even know about. We bypass them because of what he have experienced by their taste or their smell. We sometimes buy all the wrong kinds of food, but taking care of our bodies is what we should emphasize. It is funny how parents force their children to eat the right kinds of food but don't always practice what they preach. Some of the mixtures were not always tasty but I drank them anyway because they were good for my body and I was willing to try anything that was good for my health.

In my research I found out that one cancer fighting food is Pink grapefruit. One of the compounds in the grapefruit is lycopene, which is a very important antioxidant. Mushrooms suppress estrogen production in our bodies. Blueberries, strawberries and raspberries have an ellagic acid which is one of the hosts of cancer fighter. It stimulates the activity of enzymes that fight cancer growth has a group of compounds called ligans; which subdue cancerous changes once they have occurred. Celery, carrots and watercress are also cancer fighting foods. Medicines that scientists invented have a variety of side effects which can do more harm to cancer patients. Eating natural foods which are simply fruits and vegetables are enjoyable and easily prepared with no side effects. There is no need to worry about what your insurance can pay for or where you would get the money on your own to get the prescription filled. So why not try what you already know rather than take something unnatural where you have no clue of the ingredients that are in it. What do you have to lose? It does no harm to try Mother Nature's produce. Try something which can nourish and cure your body at the same time.

The morning of my appointment with the Radiology doctor. I got up prayed, had a light breakfast, and then left the house to meet Alton at his job. It took us less than an hour to get there. On our arrival I registered my name at the front desk then was told to go to the basement because that is where the department is situated. We were both welcomed by a smiling receptionist who took my name and told me to have a seat. Again there were light refreshments on a table behind us we both helped ourselves to a cold drink. A few minutes later the nurse came and called my name. We both followed her into a small room where I changed into a hospital gown she took my vital signs. Soon after, a doctor came in and introduced himself. He started asking questions because he said that he went over my medical files but the head doctor would come in and explain things to us. We waited for about another ten minutes before the head doctor came in and talked to us. She said exactly the same thing that the oncologist said to us which was based on my report. It was not useful for me to start the treatment because it would not do me any good. She told me that I should see the surgeon, that maybe there was no need to take the breast out, but the surgeon would have to make that decision, she referred me her. Everything was moving fast which meant that the hospital was on top of things; they were not wasting any time at all. I left the room with great confidence and assurance that they knew exactly what they were doing, although I was hearing the same report over and over again. It seemed like I would be losing my breast but I was not ready to give up my breast without a fight. I believe that there would be some other alternatives and that God will work it out.

THE BATTLE ZONE

My appointment for the surgeon was scheduled to be in two days. She was also a female, along with the oncologist, and radiologist. I felt lucky to have all female doctors so they would understand exactly what I was going through and how I was feeling. There are a variety of doctors who are appointed to you when you have cancer, each of them specialize in different areas of cancer. First, you meet with a Medical Oncologist who is specialized in diagnosis and general treatment. Second is the Radiation oncologist- this doctor specializes in radiation treatment for cancer. He or she formulates a safe treatment plan for each cancer patient and treats any side effects that may arise from the radiation process. Third is the Surgical Oncologist –this surgeon operates on cancer patients, performing biopsies to positively diagnose the presence of cancer and surgeries to remove tumor growths. They all work closely together to supervise the entire process. The Plastic surgeon comes in depending on your need if you were to have to reconstruction done. Overall there were four doctors involved in my cancer care at the NYU Cancer Institute whereas at the other hospital there were only two doctors the surgeon and the radiologist. Each of these doctors serves their purpose in the area that they are specialized in. The best thing about it is that they all work together to accomplish what needs to be done; which is getting rid of the cancer and bringing the patient back to good health.

Because the surgeon was a female, she knew how I was feeling about the whole cancer ordeal. She was very soft spoken. The best thing she could have said to us was that there was no need to take my breast off because of modern technology. She said that she would not recommend the silicone for me but she would highly recommend me to have the fatty tissues from my body placed, into my breast so that the size would remain the same as the other. She explained to us that she would remove most of the tissues, from the infected breast. So I would definitely be a candidate for reconstruction. She recommended a plastic surgeon that she worked closely with on the upper east side of Manhattan I was scheduled for an MRI and also a mammogram before the surgery. Things were beginning to work in my favor. I no longer needed a mastectomy but rather I was having my breast rebuilt and it felt good to know what was about to take place. She further went on to explain that I should not be concerned about payment for the reconstruction but that it was necessary and that she would contact the insurance company, asking for approval, in which they always approved

Alton and I left the doctor's office with satisfaction. Although I was about to have my third surgery I felt that I could trust these doctors. They knew what was happening to my body and how it could be dealt with. They were also my counselors. They gave me assurance that everything would be fine and I need not worry. The cancer would be taken care of. The next day I went to see the plastic surgeon; I was amazed to see how luxurious the office was. I had to double check my appointment card to make sure that I was at the correct address. It was such a beautiful office with a face- friendly secretary sitting opposite to a big glass door at the front. We said good morning to each other then I gave her my name along with my insurance card and my co-payment. I took a seat on a white leather sofa. I kept looking around because I had never seen a doctor's office more beautiful and highly decorated than that. I was observing every area and everyone at the corners of my eyes, wondering how much money was put out to the architect and the interior design team to have an outcome like that, not that it was any of my business. I was just curious.

I was distracted from my thoughts by a young Latino nurse who called my name and escorted me to the back where the examination rooms were. I took my regular clothes off and slipped into the gown with the opening to the front sat on a chair and waited patiently for the arrival of the doctor. As I waited, my eyes again started wondering all over as everything was so neatly placed in the appropriate places. I looked at the photographs of before and after reconstruction surgery which were on the wall. I was fascinated when I saw the difference. The reconstructed breast will always be more lifted than the other no matter how you age. I was pleased to know that in a few weeks that same thing would be done to me. I was excited. It did not bother me to tell anyone that I was scheduled to have reconstructive surgery. It meant that I would still have my breast it would be firmer and rounder than before, with high pointed nipples. I Nicole Lineszy was about to have new reconstructed breast.

The doctor came into the room with a bright smile on his face as if we had known each other before. He introduced himself; he sat on a chair behind the desk which was in front of me. He was silent for a minute as he looked through my medical records, then he examined me and took pictures of both breasts. The surgeon, he said, wanted him to do a flap instead of the silicone because I would be a good candidate. He further went on to explain that he would use the fatty tissues from my back, under my bra line, and that there was no need to worry because the scar would eventually be invisible. He said after the surgeon removed the cancer cells from my breast, he would come in and perform the reconstruction. The process should take approximately four to five hours.

My right breast was far different from the other due to the two surgeries that I had before. I know that this may sound crazy, but to me it looked like some sort of alien with half of a face. Half of it was gone and it bothered me every time I looked in the mirror to see what cancer had done to me.

There were a few things that needed to be done before the surgery. I was to have a pretest which I did, like all the other surgeries. Next, I had to go to the billing department and clarify how the co-payments were to be made.

The Battle Zone

As always, the night before the surgery we prayed for good and speedy recovery and that the doctors would do their best to do what needed to be done. The surgery was scheduled to be performed at 10.00am but we got there at 8.00 am. We were called into the surgical area where both doctors came in and explained what needed to be done. First there was the surgeon oncologist, and then came the plastic surgeon. He demonstrated his procedure on my breast with a marker. He marked every area that he would be working on. When they both finished, they left the room wishing me good luck. Within fifteen minutes I was parting from my husband telling him that the next time I see him I would be cancer free. I was wheeled into the theater by a nurse. She suggested that on entering the room I say a friendly hello, with a smile on my face, then introduce myself. It sounded good to me so I did like I was instructed. I introduced myself to all those who were in the room and they all greeted me, also with the same hospitality. The environment was very relaxing with soft Jazz music coming from somewhere in the room. That was the place that made us feel relaxed before going into surgery it took your mind off the bad and helped us focus on the good. The music was not only good for the patients but also for the doctors and nurses, it keeps everyone relaxed.

I was half awake when I opened my eyes and discovered that I had been wheeled by two nurses into a room which was supposed to be my home for the next two days. I tried to move my upper body while I was transferred from one bed to another, but I was so stiff that I was of no use to myself. My right breast was completely covered with bandages and so was the right portion of my back where the doctor had removed the fatty tissue. I could not keep my eyes open for long. I was still sedated.

The next time I opened my eyes, my husband Alton was at my bed side asking how I was feeling and saying that the surgery was a success. This time around, I smiled and said to myself: "Thank you, Jesus." As I looked around, I saw that I was connected to two different machines. One was monitoring my heart rate the other was hooked to antibiotics with a bag of drips. There were two bags right under the area of surgical area which were to collect all of the excess fluids. I looked down to see what my breast looked like but they were in bandages and very swollen. My body felt like I had been in a fight the night before. It was late in the afternoon and I knew that Alton was tired from such a long day so we both decided that he should go home and get some rest. Besides, I was exhausted. He left promising to be back first thing in the morning. I had dinner from what the nurse fed me, then I fell asleep.

Early the next morning the nurse gave me a sponge bath. I was uncomfortable with someone other than my husband, or my mother, cleaning my private parts but I could not help myself. Therefore she had to do what needed to be done. The doctor's made their visit, asked how I was feeling, then told me the date of my follow up. Breakfast was served and I ate it all because I was hungry and it tasted good. My comfort was the television. Alton had ordered the package so that I would not be bored. Ever so often he called to find out how I was feeling. I was honest by telling him exactly how sore I was. He said that he would be there as soon as he could. I told him there was no need to rush over because his sisters had just walked into the room and if I needed help in any kind of way they would assist. His sisters and I both talked about the surgery and how the hospital staff was very loving and caring. If I knew about them before, I would have gone to them instead of the other hospital.

It was early July 2010, so we talked about how hot the weather was outside but the hospital room was very cool. I had no problem with the outside heat. They both stayed for a while and we all enjoyed each others company. I was happy to have visitors at my side. When Alton walked it was a delight to see him. My family was at my side and nothing mattered at that time. I laid in bed looking and listening to each and everyone of them, talking and making jokes. They all get along well as brothers and sisters. The girls respected their brother Alton for whom he was.

At the end of the day I felt weary and everyone left so I decided to get some rest. The next day, I was going to be discharge. Alton was there early. He was able to help me into my clothes while the nurse went to get all my discharged instructions. She instructed me carefully that I was not allowed to get the surgical parts of my body wet until I had a follow up with the doctors. Someone from the Visiting Nurse Services assigned me to a program to have a visiting nurse come to my house. Two nights away from my home seemed like two months, I wanted to be home in my own bed. I left the hospital that afternoon knowing that I had undergone the last surgery. There were no cancer surgeries for me it was over and done with I could move on with life. Nothing was going to stop me or hold me back from doing the things in life which I was passionate about. I could now breathe "Oh thank you Jesus once again."

When we arrived at the house, I changed into my pajamas again with my husband's help. While changing, I took a long look in the mirror from front to back. I stared at the bandages. I could not believe that I had just done a third surgery but it was okay because I knew that there would be no more. I walked as if I was learning to do so because of the pain and discomfort that I was in. I was unable to stand for long. I felt like I had no strength to take care of my personal needs. How long would this horrible feeling last? I asked myself once again. I took my medications to avoid any pain. I was prescribed Tylenol w/ cod#3. These were no ordinary medications because my eyes stayed opened a short time, then I fell asleep. They were designed to ease the pain but cause excess drowsiness at the same time.

Two days after I was released from the hospital my niece came from Florida to help around the house. It was a big help to have her there with me. I took two weeks away from my job and I was glad that I did that. There was no-way I could have gone back out any sooner because of the way I was feeling. Everyone called showing their care and concern. Some even came by the house to visit, bringing gifts with them. One of the sisters from church even went all the way to bring food at 9.00am. I appreciated all of the attention I was getting and wished that I could repay them all in some way, but all I could have said to each and everyone was, "Thank you." When you are in a situation like this you have to be grateful for all the help that you can get. We are living in a World today where everyone is busy either with work or in their own personal life. My Pastor was out of the country doing God's work. To my surprise, she called to find out how I was feeling. I felt her love just knowing that she took the time off to call to know how I was progressing. It was good to know that so many people cared about my health.

Every morning, Alton assists in getting me out of bed because I could not do it on my own. It was extremely difficult for me, I guess because I was not moving around at nights. Sometimes it hurt my feelings to know that I had been through so much over the past months. It seemed as though when I healed from one surgery another one came along. I felt that my body was not getting enough time to recuperate and gain strength. I was going through a lot of physical and also emotional pain. I could not compare them because they both were affecting me in a great way.

The physical pain after each surgery was unbearable. Not only the pain but also the weaknesses made me not want to get out of bed. The emotional pain played tricks with my mind. One minute I would be fine, the next I would find myself in deep sadness. Sometimes when someone asked how I was doing I would say that I was doing great. However it was a lie. I was hurting deep inside, Yet I had a smile on my face pretending that I was doing great. I was hiding my emotional pain well without anyone noticing.

Sometimes I hated talking about cancer because it brought sadness to my heart. It was a good thing when wasn't questioned about it. When talking to a cancer victim the supporters, should be very careful of what they say to that person. You shouldn't say things like "Oh, I know someone who died of the disease" or "I hear that the treatment is awful." Those comments burden the cancer victim with negative thoughts. You must always speak positively to that person concerning their health. If you have no positive words to say to a person who has cancer, just do not say anything because the wrong words can do harm to that person. We the victims, know that you care about our health but we don't want the negative feedback from you. In life there are two kinds of pain. There are emotional pain and physical pain. Everyone in life at some point has experienced emotional pain, whether from losing a loved one or through separation in marriage. However, that cannot be compared with being diagnosed with a disease such as cancer, which could change your life forever. That kind of pain has a significant mental and emotional hold on you. The pain tears you up inside. Your heart is not just broken but you feel as if your soul is being ripped apart. You try to control the feeling but sometimes it wins you over. It immediately dominates

The Battle Zone

your entire body. You no longer have the desire to do the things that you used to love doing. It's as if you are placed in a box where all you can see is the problem; nothing else matters at that time not food, not work. Your happiness is snatched away from you without any questions. No amount of money in the world could bring you back that joy which was taken away from you the instant you knew that your health was compromised.

Being diagnosed with cancer can cause a lot of emotional pain both for you and your family. There are no pain killers for emotional pain. Unlike physical pain, nothing can be prescribed to ease your mental state at that particular time.

Everyone handles emotional pain differently. Some turn to drugs and alcohol, others prostitution. Even though you may think that you are strong enough to handle the pain you are going through, there must be someone you can confide in who will be able to help you overcome the problems that you are facing. They may not feel the anger and the outrage you are going through because pain is only felt by the individual. But even if they have not been through the same situation, they can help with words of encouragement. It is important to control your emotional pain so that your overall everyday performance would not be hindered. Some may get their counseling from friends or loved ones, but the only one who can get you back on your feet again is God. It is very important that you pull yourself back together when you are in an emotional state and cannot function effectively. A good positive thinking person will always win and cannot lose over any sickness. That is the attitude we must always have. Cancer victims must know that they are winners and not losers. That is the key to overcoming the diagnosis.

Three days after surgery the hospital called to know how I was doing. They asked if I was still swollen from the surgery. They mentioned that a visiting nurse would be coming to my house the next day and if I had any concerns I should let her know. I was happy to know that a professional was coming over to make sure that I was progressing the way I should. The visiting nurse did arrive at the house the next day as they said she would. She spent an hour taking my blood pressure and asking all the necessary questions about my health she complemented me on how I looked for a person who had just had surgery. I thanked her for her good remarks. She left saying that she would be back the next week at the same time, I said goodbye and thanked her for coming.

REFLECTIONS

Being diagnosed with Breast Cancer has taught me a lot about life. I have learned that life should never be taken for granted. Life should be cherished because it is our best gift from God. We must all learn to love each other and treat one another with respect regardless of the individual. Cancer makes me want to run after the good things of life. I want to do things which I have never thought I could do I want to travel the World to see different countries. I Nicole Lineszy, want to live a happy prosperous life. Cancer has improved my relationship with my friends and my family. It has also drawn me closer to God. I have learned to love and to forgive all those who have done me wrong. I have never been that scared before I was diagnosed, but I thank God everyday for being at my side. I would not have made it without his tender love, His mercy and His grace. In Trinidad where I was born, it is often said that when you have cancer you should always opt out of surgery because when you have surgery on a tumor air gets to it, which allows it to spread elsewhere and grows rapidly. That concerned me because of the many surgeries I had before and still could not get a negative pathology reading. But whatever led me to have three surgeries, I am very thankful and grateful that I made it through and can now counsel others who are now battling with the disease.

REALITY

Cancer can break you or it can build you up. The disease brought me to my knees on several occasions but I found strength inside of me. Cancer was not just attacking my body physically but had played a drastic l effect on my marriage. It was taking over and I was allowing it. I was not acting the role of a wife anymore. I had lost my sexual desire towards my husband and there was no intimacy between us for a long time. I was being selfish thinking only about myself and not the needs of my husband. He felt alone in the marriage. He said to me one day he understood my pain but I needed to let him into my emotions as well. He said that we were in this together and I was not alone. I knew deep down that he was 100% correct. I was acting like the disease had the best of me and I was not allowing him to reach out to me the way he wanted to. It was very hard for me to think intimacy when I was still dealing with Cancer. I was still going through the physical and the emotional stress that came along with cancer. My body was going through changes. After I had the second surgery, half of my breast was missing sometimes I would be embarrassed to look at myself much more to let my husband look at me. After the third surgery there were no feelings in my right breast; it felt numb and still is today but I have gotten over the changes. Cancer was just not destroying me but it was interfering with my marriage and I hated it.

It is very difficult for friends and family to understand the torment that a woman goes through when she is told that she has Cancer. They expect you to snap right out of your emotions and come back to reality, but it is a process that you must go through.

EMPOWERMENT

There are six steps that a cancer victim goes through when diagnosed. They are very scared that they will lose their life or scared that cancer may over throw them because they may have heard many times that cancer can be fatal. You ask yourself "Why me? "Or "What did I do wrong?" Some people do believe that they are being punished for something that they did in their past.

Second: You are in denial. You cannot believe that the horrible disease is now a part of you. It is very difficult to accept what is now a part of your life. It takes some time for you to adjust to the fact that you been have given a cancer diagnosis. You are still in shock and disbelief.

Third: Depression. You no longer have the desire for the things which you once loved to do. Nothing matters to you anymore and you go into a place of frustration.

Fourth bargain. This is the point where you tell God that you would do anything He wants you to do so that you could be healthy. If you never believed in Christ, your cancer diagnosis will most certainly bring you to that place in Him where they have no other choice but to trust Him completely.

Fifth acceptance: You feel that cancer does not have a strong hold on you anymore. You are no longer living in fear. Denial and depression have all disappeared and you are filled with strength from God to fight for life.

Sixth resurrection. You may now have the faith that you have prayed so desperately for, because you want to live and take control over life again. You have the power over what once controlled your life. You are stronger and have the knowledge which you once lacked.

Cancer is not a punishment for things that you thought you may have done wrong in your life. It is no one's fault. Every cancer victim handles their diagnosis differently. Some, like me, say that the experience has improved the quality of their lives. It is not a sign of weakness to express your emotions. Many people go through a time of grief and sadness when they first learn about their diagnosis. That it is a normal response to a profound change in a person's life.

It takes a lot of patience and understanding to cope with a Cancer victim who is going through so many difficult emotions. I remembered that in my early fight, I was judged by my friends because I disconnected myself from the people I used to keep in contact with. I was not calling them as I used to nor was I retuning or answering their calls when they did try to reach out to me. They thought that maybe I was not interested in their friendship anymore. When I told them about the Cancer, they apologized with their deepest regrets for what I was going through. It is not that you don't what to involve the people that are in your life but the last thing you want is to be felt sorry for. It adds to the stress because some people look at you with only sorrow on their faces instead of building you up with encouragement. But sharing your diagnosis when you don't know what step to take next can be rewarding in a sense. Someone may refer you to a good doctor who specializes in that area and can save your life .They may also suggest some sort of medicine that can help you along the way but most of all, their prayers can resurrect and keep you strong to fight the battle.

It's a struggle to deal with cancer. The process can be longer than expected. It is not over until you have the final treatment therapy. Depending on your diagnosis it can take a year to get through the process. If you are a strong person you can overcome the emotions that are involved quickly, but some take longer than others and may have to seek professional help.

I thank God everyday that I did not lose my sanity, but instead I became a stronger woman as the process went by. September 2011 will be my first birthday after being Cancer free. I did my first Cancer walk in October 2010. I did it with my husband, his sister and a dear friend of mine. We, the Cancer victims, along with our friends and family all met at Prospect Park early one Sunday morning. I had never seen so many women coming together to fight for what was right and that is "The cure". We need to find a cure to put cancer to a stop. There were women of all cultures and ages all reaching out to show love towards each other.

My advice to all females is to please have a mammogram done yearly. Examine your breasts daily. Saving your life starts with you. Don't wait until it's too late. Start today. This is my cry to all my sisters out there. Remind a friend or take a friend with you. Let it be a girly day with you and someone. Make it a happy fun and interesting event. You may both thank each other one day. Cancer is one of the leading causes of death among African American women today, so we have to take charge of our lives. We have to eat healthy meals and do our exercises, but most importantly, we have to start getting our screening every year. It is for our best.

Being strong spiritually has a big impact on how you manage cancer. Once you are in Christ, you have to trust and depend on him for your healing. He is the one that heals you mentally so that you can overcome your physical ailment. He gives you the grace everyday to stand strong with your head held high and say boldly "I am healed" because God said so. He puts in you the power to be victorious.

Let me tell you a little about how God works. First of all, we serve a faithful God. When He says that He is going to do something (heal your sick body) He does. He does not go back on His word. I would encourage you to read the book of John from beginning to end and see all the miraculous marvelous work that Christ did. Remember, if He did it then, He would most certainly do it for you in this life time. Trust and believe God and never ever give up on your life, or on God.

A week after the surgery, I went to the surgeon to have a follow up. She removed the bandages to get a clear view of the breast. Everything looked wonderful she said, and then she replaced the bigger bandage with a smaller one.

I also had an appointment with the plastic surgeon for the following week. While I was in the waiting area I noticed a lady with her face all bandaged up and I said to myself maybe she had a face lift. There were also other patients, all with different problems from the way they all looked. The nurse called my name and I followed her into the examination room where the doctor came in and looked at the surgical breast. He was satisfied to see how quickly the scars were healing. There was a lot of fluid in the drainage bag so he replaced them the with an empty one and disconnected the smaller bag because I no longer needed it. He asked if I was in any pain. I had just a little discomfort. He looked at the other surgical area on my back and removed the bandage and few of the stitches and said that the rest would dissolve on their own. My next visit with him would be in a week's time again.

When I got home from my doctor's appointment, I was very exhausted. I felt a lot of pulling across my back from the scar, so I decided to get some rest. I felt challenged at times when taking care of my physical needs. I depended on the help from others. I felt disabled but I was only doing what was right for my health. Straining to do the daily chores would only do harm to my body. Resting would be part of the healing process. I needed lots of it so I took advantage of the situation and went along with the doctor's orders.

As the days went by, I started to feel stronger. I was doing the things which I could not have done a few days earlier. The visiting nurse came on her second visit, asked how I was doing and took notes. She also took my vital signs and everything looked normal. She looked at the breast and the drainage bag said that there was not much fluid in it and that on my next doctor's visit he would remove it. We set a date and a time for the next visit then she left. A Couple of days after, I got mail from the Visiting Nurse Service. To my surprise it there was a bill stating that I had owed the company $30.00 for the first visit. I was stunned because no one told me that I had to pay for the services. I thought that they were covered under my insurance. This means that there would be a second bill coming. I called the agency and I cancelled all of their services. A few days after someone from the Cancer Society called to offer a free wig which I gladly excepted. They made the arrangements for someone to come over to the house at my convenience. She asked what styles of wig I like straight, curly, long or short. She also said that if I did not like the ones she showed me, there would be a catalog where I could choose from and they would have one ordered. The organization offers free wigs to cancer patients. It was very pleasing to know that they cared so much about us.

Friends and family were still calling to know about my progress. One week later, I was back to see the plastic surgeon for another follow up. This was the second one since the surgery. He removed the drainage bag which I was happy to have taken off. He looked at my breast and everything was fine. I was swollen and he instructed me to continue wearing a support bra. I looked at myself in the mirror, I saw the scars on my breast and the other on my back and felt a bit embarrassed to see how cancer had changed my appearance. The doctor said that the scars would fade away after a period of time. But it does not matter how faded the scar may get, there will always be two permanent scars remaining with me for the rest of my life. The first is the memory of what I went through with breast cancer the other is the physical scar on my body. Every time I looked in the mirror, I will always remembered that I was a victim of breast cancer. Those are the scars that I will never forget so long as I have life. Sometimes, when I undressed myself, I avoid looking in the mirror, afraid to face the damages that cancer did to my body. I hid the scars from my husband for a long period of time until I eventually got used to them.

RADIATION THERAPY

As time went by I started juicing and cooking healthy meals to help get through a speedy recovery from the surgery. I was building my immune system to help withstand the radiation therapy that I was about to start in a few weeks. My strength felt restored as the weeks went by. I decided to go to church so that I could thank God for keeping me alive after everything I had been through. Cancer had a strong hold on me but God kept me alive for a reason. Many of my church family were happy for my progress and I was happy to be in the house of the Lord.

The oncologist was happy to see the progress I made since after the surgery and even happier to know that the surgery was a success. She examined the surgical area on my breast and was satisfied that it was healing without any problems. She discussed with my husband and I the medication that I would be placed on after the radiation therapy was over which would be tamoxifen. She went on to explain that I would be on the pill for five years and that I should not consider pregnancy because of the risk of damage to the fetus. She went on to explain the different side effects of the medication.

Tamoxifen is used to block the effects of estrogen. It is commonly used to treat breast cancer. It is also use to decrease the chance of returning breast cancer in women who had received treatment for the disease.

Some side effects of using tamoxifen are as follows:

* changes in vision.
* Changes in your menstrual.
* Difficulty breathing or shortness of breath.
* Difficulty walking or talking.
* Pelvic pain or pressure.
* Hot flashes.
* Uterine cancer.

   The doctor also said that a pap smear should be done yearly to detect any changes in my uterus. If there is any change I should consult with her. I was hesitant as to whether or not to take tamoxifen, because of the many side effects. It seemed like the drug could do more harm than good. The thought still lingers in me. Why do scientists invent these drugs that can add to our problems? But I put my trust completely in God that my body will not to be affected with any side effects.

   As it drew nearer to start of the radiation therapy (It has been six weeks already since I had the surgery and that was the waiting period for the healing to take place),I began to get nervous because of the expectations. The morning of the appointment the radiologist team (doctor and nurse) took time to explain the procedure step by step. The treatment would be for five weeks, five days per week. The treatment is approximately 20-25 minutes, depending on the technicians. Someone had to be present with me during the first week of treatment in case of any nausea. She went on to say that I should expect some discoloration on my breast during the treatment but that could be taken care of with a special lotion which would be given to me later on in the process. She also said that my husband would be given a free ticket for valet parking. The doctors used a patient who was on her final treatment as an example to let me know what to expect. The patient said that the physical feeling was painless and there was nothing to be worried about, but at times I may feel a little tired. There was relief to know that there was no pain involved during the treatment. After our discussion the doctor wished me good luck, then I went over to the other side of the corridor where I begin my first step of the radiation therapy. The nurse introduced herself and told me that she would be my technician each time I came for treatment, along with two other male technicians whom I was yet to meet. She showed me a few lockers where I would keep my personal belongings each time that I came for treatment.

I did as I was told, then I followed her into the radiation room where I met with the other technicians. They were polite, patient and friendly. They opened a door and led me inside a huge room with a bed which was about six feet long and approximately four feet high with a circle to the top and on the right semi circle. The bed was surrounded by a huge machine. Two of the technicians assisted in getting me on the high bed. I felt embarrassed exposing my scarred breast to the two technicians because they were male. They said that I should lie flat on my stomach. It took them a few minutes to get my body positioned the correct way. They made a lot of markings on my back which would remain permanent after the five weeks of treatment. After the markings on my back were placed, they all left the room and instructed me that I should not move until I was told to do so.

Besides the noisy machine, all I could hear coming from the room was one of the technicians telling me to breathe in at one point, then she would say" breath out". They took a lot of x-rays of the breast where the cancer was located. The doctor looked at it and gave her approval. That was all that I had done for the day until the actual treatment itself where I would have to meet with the nurse, I got dressed and went to the other side of the room to discuss my schedule. They explained at the end of each week that the x-ray procedure will be repeated.

On my way out, I stopped at the nurse's station to set up a date and a time when I would be coming for the treatments. Early morning was the schedule I chose because it was convenient to me. It did not matter what day of the week I started, as long as I did five consecutive days. I asked what if I missed a dose and she said that I could always do a makeup but I should try not to have missed days. My schedule was Wednesdays through Sundays. Each day the treatment was to begin at 8.00 am. After the treatment there would have enough time to relax before going to work. When I was through making the appointments, I left the cancer center thinking that it would be all over soon. As much as I wanted the treatment to be over with, I did not want the side effects which would make me tired, so I kept a positive attitude about that.

Radiation therapy or radiotherapy is defined as a treatment which kills cancer cells remaining in the body after surgery. This type of therapy is well tolerated by many patients. The side effects that you may experience are as follows:

: Skin reaction -the area affected may appear reddened or burned, you may have itchiness or peeling.
: Pain or discomfort in the chest or armpit area.

: Low white blood cell count.

: Fatigue-the treatment may also affect your lungs and your heart. That is why at the NYU Cancer Center, the treatment is given to you lying flat on your stomach. In that way the chances of the treatment getting to your heart or lungs are slight.

The First day of the actual radiotherapy treatment

Alton was with me because the doctor suggested that it would be a good idea to have someone with me in case of any nauseous feelings and also he wanted to be there to give his love and support. We drove into Manhattan because now he was entitled to free valet parking. It took us approximately 45 minutes to get there, which was not too bad seeing that we had run into traffic on the way down. Alton drove up in front of the hospital, showed the valet guys our parking ticket, and they took the car. The radiatiotherapy room was located at the basement of the hospital. As we entered the room, the receptionist recognized me and she said, "Good morning, Ms Lineszy. "How are you?" I waited 15 minutes, then the nurse called my name. I followed her to the room where I changed and put my belongings into the locker. I had a key with a wrist band around it so that I could keep it with me at all times. After a few minutes of getting undressed the nurse called my name a second time. This time with a much softer tone because she knew then exactly who I was, so there was no need to shout for me.

I followed her into the radiation room where I greeted the other two technicians, who directed me to room where I became fully undressed. They assisted me to get onto the bed into the correct position which I had done the week before. The green beaming lights were now green but when turned on, switched to red. When I was in the correct position, the technicians told me not to move, the treatment was about to begin. They left the room, leaving me with the enormous machine which sounded like a robot in action. I did nothing but pray. I asked God to let the treatment be a success, let it do what it was supposed to do without destroying my white blood cells. Before I could get comfortable on the bed, the treatment was all over. The technicians came in told me I did great, and asked how I was feeling which was not any different from the way I came in. They helped me off the bed, and said that they would see me the next day for my next treatment. They said before I left the building, I would have to stop by the radiotherapy oncologist to do a follow up since it was my first treatment and she would want to know how my body tolerated it.

When I got to her, she asked how I was feeling and said if there were any changes in my health during the treatment I should consult with her immediately. She also reminded me that as time went by I would see some discoloration on my breast which was normal. I went back to where I kept my belongings, changed into my clothes, then I went to the waiting room where my husband was sitting. He seemed happy to see me again and asked how I was feeling. I said fine, we left the basement and went to get the car from the valet parking out front. I went to work that day feeling my normal self.

The first week of the treatment went by quickly. I did not have any side effects. Everything looked the same. There was no darkening of my breast, nor was I feeling any extra tiredness. I did the same routine everyday: I arrived at the cancer center, I went to the basement registered my name, waited to be called, went in and changed, waited to be called again, then went into the room where the treatment would begin. The treatment lasted 15 minutes. During my treatment period, I adopted a new habit which was shopping. Every day, I would go to the department stores in Manhattan and buy things that I wanted rather than needed. Shopping kept my mind clear. I felt emotionally free when I shopped. My husband was not complaining about my shopping because he wanted me to be happy after everything I had been through. He did not mind that I was treating myself and doing what made me happy, I was glad that he tolerated my spending habits.

The second week came and still I was not having any side affects. I remained happy about that, I was in for my treatment and out in 15 minutes. At the end of the weekly, I visited the doctor for a routine check for any health changes. There was no need for Alton to come to the treatments with me because I was not having any nauseous feelings, so I did the traveling back and forth on my own.

FREE AT LAST

The next three weeks came by and that is when I started to see a difference in my skin color. It looked like I was getting a tan on my breast. The nurses gave me a bottle of lotion to help with the discoloration. As the days went by the discoloration grew worse. It went all the way under my armpit. I was told that I should not use cocoa butter because the ingredients would interfere with the radiation treatment. The stitches were coming apart and that was worrying me. I was afraid that I would get an infection. My flesh was exposed and there was some discharge. I brought it to the nurses' attention the next morning and she said that everything that I was experiencing was normal during the radiation treatment. She gave me an ointment to help fight any germs because of the exposure. She also said that when I got home, I should take my bra off and expose the area to air which would help with the healing. There was no need to discontinue the treatment so the technicians continued.

A few days later my breast started to get worse in color; it was getting darker and darker and it started peeling. It was horrible to look at. The lotion was not working well; I was still using it hoping that one day it would. As the days went by, I started to experience a tired feeling. My energy level was really low and it was hard for me to keep up with my daily activities. I felt as if my body was not capable of doing any chores. I would rather lie in bed all day long. I started falling asleep during working hours and that was something that had never happened to me. I was not taking my daily vitamins because I was told not to during treatment it would interact with the doses of the radiation treatment. I was trying to get my energy from a daily Red Bull or Lucozade. My husband was buying me Ensure by the cases, to help maintain my body fat during the treatment. Each day I drank at least three of them to maintain my weight.

The following week, which was the fourth, I started to get very anxious knowing that there was only one more week of treatment left and it would all be over with. The discoloration on my breast was still there and there was nothing I could do to prevent it. The good thing was that I was not in any pain. I had made friends with a couple of people and they were all experiencing the same problem with their breast that I was having. Some were even worse than mine. I believed that after the five weeks of treatments was over the discoloration would still be there for a while, so I bought a container of yellow cocoa butter to lighten the dark area after the treatment was all over with.

Radiotherapy started to affect my skin and my overall performance in many ways, yet I was happy that the doctors did not recommend chemotherapy which would have been worse on my health. There was no hair on my armpit due to the damage that the treatment was causing on my skin. One Sunday I missed a dosage because I felt sick on my way to Manhattan. I called the cancer center and they said that I could always do a makeup day which meant that I would have one extra day on my schedule. I called my husband to get me as soon as I reached a Brooklyn stop. He came and took me home.

The next day I felt much better so I continued with the treatment. As I started to mark the days, I counted the remainder. I was scheduled to see the plastic surgeon one afternoon after the radiation treatment for a follow up. He looked at the darkened area of the breast and was not surprised. He told me that I needed a little repair after the treatment was over because the right side of the breast needed to be brought out a little to match the left one. It was too early to tell if there would be any changes in the size because radiation treatment also causes some shrinkage of the breast. I was not going to have any more surgeries done on my breast. I had been through enough already. My breast looked perfectly fine to me. My husband was not complaining, I knew that the doctor just only wanted to have a well finished job but I was satisfied with the way I looked, and nothing, or no-one, could convince me to change my mind.

The fifth week was finally here and I have been waiting for it for a long time. I never felt happier during my treatment. I knew that in a few days it would be over and I would be looking back to say to myself or to someone out there, "I made it through cancer and the treatment therapy that came with it. I did not do it by myself but with the help of God, my medical team, my friends and my family." It was a journey not only for me but for my husband. Cancer was an experience we both will never forget. The disease itself has taught us about life and its unexpected changes. I have learned so much about the disease and what can be done to prevent it, as well as the actual treatment itself and how it could affect someone's overall performance. I will always be grateful to everyone who gave their support and to our heavenly Father for bringing me through the rough times. The nurses and the technicians were all very supportive and caring. They said that I should come visit them whenever I have a follow up with the doctors. I will certainly miss them all.

On the last day of the treatment, I bought a thank you card and a box of chocolate for the technicians who were with me from the beginning to the end. I wanted to cry for joy to know that I made it through breast cancer. I had my health back so there was no stopping me now. I was going to fulfill my dreams. I was about to take back everything that the enemy thought he stole from me. I know that God is on my side so who could be against me? I was ready to relive my life, this time with a purpose. I felt like screaming, jumping and wailing; Cancer is no longer with me. It is over and done with because of the goodness of God. It was my celebration time.

I can now confess to the world that I was once a victim of breast cancer. The diagnosis was terrifying and very emotional for me and my family but I got through it. If I can overcome cancer and so can you. I know exactly how you feel when you first get the news, but as time goes by you must pull yourself together as quickly as possible and put all of your trust in God. You must learn how to fight for your life and make it your resolution everyday to want to live not- just for yourself but remember, your loved ones need you. So keep a positive mindset about cancer. It does not matter what stage you may be in, know that you are a winner. Know that your life is not over until God says it's over. It does not matter what the doctors may say about your medical report, they are only doing their job. This is your life and you cannot give up. Fight for it.

During my ordeal, I placed scriptures in each room of my apartment to remind myself of God's promises. Every day I arose I said to myself I am not sick because I am already healed in the name of Jesus, or I would say, by his stripes I am healed, I recited those phrases every day. Someone once told me that a woman sick with cancer for a long time and every day her sister would pray asking God to please heal her sister from cancer. Her prayers were not answered because eventually her sick sister died. The woman was very upset with God for not healing her sister from cancer as she begged him daily to do. Then God answered her by saying, "Everyday you have asked me to heal your sister but I did answer your prayers from the very first day". The lesson that we must learn is how to redirect our prayers by practicing our faith in God and understanding that He has already said yes to all of our prayers from the very first day. It is our time to act out in faith and believe the impossible.

A month after the treatment was over I had an appointment with the oncologist. She congratulated me on finishing the treatment. The darkened area on my breast was beginning to fade, but slowly. Everything else was in good condition and there was no need for me to see her again. Therefore I was discharged from the radiology department. I visited the surgeon and she was happy to know that I was finished with the treatment. She said that I would need a mammogram every six months. This was mandatory for anyone after being diagnosed with breast cancer. She made an appointment so that I could have one done in December. She also said that I would have to see her every six months to monitor my progress. My visit with the oncologist is scheduled for every six months as well so that she could monitor my health and assess how I am coping with tamoxifen.

The next appointment on my agenda was with the plastic surgeon. He was pleased to see that the scars were healing nicely but he still mentioned the idea of having a minor surgery to do the repairs that were needed on my breast. I said that if ever I changed my mind, I should come to see him. Other than that, there was no need for a visit with him again.

MY REBIRTH

*E*arly November, after my cancer treatment ended, I started to write this book about my ordeal. I wanted to inspire someone who may now be facing breast cancer and cannot come to terms with the disease. I also wanted the world to know what it is like to be a cancer victim. Another reason I wrote this book is to prove to myself that I can do anything I put my heart and mind to. I had full confidence that when I came up with the idea of writing my cancer story, I could do it with God's help. I told myself that I would not be disqualified. I can do all things through Christ who strengthens me and be successful in doing it.

Whitney Houston sang a song, "I didn't know my own strength," which I love. Breast cancer took me to a place where I found the strength I thought I never had. I fell, I tumbled down but I did not crumble; I got up through all the pain. I shed a lot of tears. I doubted myself. I was angry and frustrated but I got through all the pain. I am so much stronger today than when I was first diagnosed.

I eventually told my mother the truth, after everything was over. She cried, knowing that she was not present with me in my time of need. My husband and I convinced her that we were only doing what was best by keeping the truth from her. She understood. She forgave us both. I am happy to know that there are no more secrets. I know that I left my mother out by not telling her what was happening to my health. She would have wanted to be right at my side all the way to the end, giving her love and support just like everyone else. Now that I know that I am cancer free and healthy, she deserves to know the truth. I did not disclose my secret over the phone but Alton and I made a trip down to Trinidad where we told her the truth.

DISAPPOINTMENT

One year after my surgery, I was scheduled to have another mammogram. My husband and I just came from a Canadian cruise. We were still very excited. It was our first cruise as a married couple and it was much more fun than we originally thought. The appointment for the checkup was two days after my trip and I kept it although I knew that I would still be overwhelmed from having had such a wonderful time. I had an afternoon appointment. I arrived at the NYU Cancer Center in enough time to fill the necessary paper work. When my turn came, I went into the examination room, got undressed from my waist up and waited for the nurse to escort me to the room where she would perform the procedure. Having a mammogram is painful but I was used to it by then.

The test was over and I waited for the results which would normally take forty-five minutes to one hour. Within a few minutes of my wait, the nurse called me in the examination room again because she needed to repeat the mammogram on the right breast. Again, I waited until I was called by the doctor who then told me that there were some calcification in my right breast which needed further testing. Not again, I said to myself. Why do I have to go through this ordeal every time? Then I started praying silently. The doctor gave me an appointment to have a needle biopsy in a few days. I tried to stay as calm as possible as I left the building.

The previous ordeal that I had been through soon started playing in my head. I tried to override it with good thoughts. I waited until I reached home to explain to my husband that I needed further testing. He did not panic and neither did I. We kept a positive mindset, believing that everything was going to be just fine. The doctor was simply taking precautions to making sure that my body was functioning the way it was supposed to.

The morning of the biopsy I was a little nervous due to the fact that the previous one was uncomfortable. But, this one was different. I was placed on my stomach with my right breast in a hole from a bed, so the machine could work on me from below. The procedure took about 30 minutes. I was given another appointment to see my doctor in one week. Although I felt a little sore, I was convinced that I was going to be just fine.

The morning of my appointment I wanted to hear nothing but good news. But there was a turn around with my report. The doctor said that the calcification meant that cancer was still present in my breast. She went on to explain that since I had already gotten radiology the only thing to do was to remove the right breast. I took it better than I thought I would. She said that the left breast was not a problem but I suggested that she remove them both. I was tired enough of cancer already. When would it stop completely? I wanted to have a bilateral mastectomy. That way I would not have to worry ever again about breast cancer. I knew that I was making the right decision not only for my life but also for my family. They would not have to see me go through all the pain and headache anymore.

The doctor did not agree but she said if that was what I wanted then she would respect my decision. We discussed the necessary steps which were seeing the plastic surgeon to talk about the reconstruction and having a bone scan to test for any spreading of the cancer. I was surprised by how soon she wanted the procedure done. I thought that maybe it could have waited just a few months because I started a new semester of studies only a week ago. I mentioned that I was in school; her opinion was for me to stop all classes as soon as possible. Her secretary wrote me a letter to the school explaining that I had to drop all classes, due to an emergency surgery.

On my way home, I called my husband telling him what needed to be done. He respected my decision and said that he would support me in any way that he could. He was fine with me not having any breast at all if it meant saving my life. I told him about breast reconstruction. We both phoned our family, including my mother, to

Disappointment

inform them about what was happening. They all supported my decision. I went to bed that night feeling convinced that I had made the right decision for my health. I felt excited by the thought of having implants. I knew then what I did not know in the past- that most women who have had breast cancer had made the same decision, and it had all turned out for the best. I also learned that women today are removing their breasts even just to save themselves the trouble of having to go through the ordeal of cancer.

The bone scan was a long, nerve wrecking process but it turned out that the cancer had not invaded any other parts of my body. That was great news to the doctor, my husband and me. On my visit with the plastic surgeon, he mentioned that the reconstruction would look like my natural breasts, I was happy to hear that the outcome would be great. I started to prepare myself for the surgery by doing a lot of meditation. I also kept busy so I would not be thinking too much about the surgery. I had the full support of both my family and friends and that gave me good encouragement. I was not fighting the cancer fight alone but I had many strong people on my side. I did a lot of organizing at home making sure that my husband knew where everything important was. I also did a lot of arrangements in our closets because the fall season was right around the corner and stretching up high would be impossible for me after the surgery. I had everything that I needed. The day the surgery was drawing near. I was ready to get it over with but there was still a feeling inside of me that I could not explain. I was about to lose both of my natural breasts, to never see or feel them again. They were to be replaced by what man has created instead of what God had given me. I took as many pictures as I could so that I would always have a remembrance of what my natural breasts looked like before the reconstruction.

The morning before I left the house to go to the hospital, I took a long look in the mirror at both breasts. I held them in my hands in a final goodbye. It hurt deep inside although I knew that everything was going to be just fine. My cousin came from North Carolina the night before to give her support for which made me very happy. My aunt from New Jersey met us at the hospital the day of the surgery.

We left the house at five that morning. We made a short stop by my friend's house. She was going to be there to give her support also. As we drove to the hospital we talked about everything except the surgery. The music in the car was also very relaxing. The roads were clear and it took only a short time to arrive at the hospital. There, three doctors- the cancer surgeon, the plastic surgeon and the anesthesiologist- explained their procedures to us. The surgeon's job was to remove the breast then the plastic surgeon would put in the tissue expanders. The entire procedure would take approximately four hours. My family and I held hands and prayed before I went into the operating room. As I walked into the theater, the doctors and the nurses greeted me warmly, one of the nurses guided me to the table with all the equipment. I laid and immediately they connected my body with the various machines, the anesthesiologist placed the needles in my arms and I fell into a deep sleep.

When I awoke I was surrounded by my loved ones in the recovery room. I was happy to see them although I felt like I was not 100% awake. But they seemed to be much happier. They stayed with me for a few minutes in the recovery room. The surgery was over. My breasts were removed and the area where they used to be was now covered in bandages. I felt stiffness throughout my entire chest. I could not move my arms. I felt lucky to be alive. I had just come through another cancer surgery and I felt fine. The discomfort that I was having was temporary; it would go away and I would be up and about like before.

I was moved to a room on the upper floor of the hospital after I had been taken from the recovery area. All through the night my vital signs were monitored by the nurses. Early the next morning, I was awakened by the voice of the plastic surgeon. He said everything went well but there was still a lot of work to be done.

There were a lot of visitors the next day. I was very happy to see them all. After they left, the television was my companion, although I was asleep most of the time due to the pain killers I was given. The nurses came in very often, making sure that I was as comfortable as possible. The days went by quickly. I went through the same routines. There was not much the doctors could do but just look for any excess leakage. There was none; just a very swollen area. They advised me to start taking short walks. I was much more alert than the previous day. I did as I was told but during the first attempt I started getting

Disappointment

a faint feeling and had to return to my room. I was not as strong as I looked. I wished that I could have done more, but I could not, although I was able to take care of my own personal hygiene. Alton came by in the afternoon. He sat and we talked, he said that he could hardly wait for me to be home. He said I looked beautiful despite of the surgery I had just been through. The doctors said that I would be home the next day because of the speedy recovery that I was making. It was good news for us I would be home in my bed where I would be comfortable and taken special care of. Not that I was not getting the care that I needed in the hospital, but being home in your own bed is a lot different. The morning of my release from the hospital, the nurse went over all of the instructions and handed Alton a prescription for pain killers. After we finished our questions and answers with the nurse she called and ordered a wheel chair assistant to take me to the car. It was very difficult getting in and out of the car but with Alton's help, I managed. When we got to the house I took the valium and ox cyclone. I was used to taking those strong pain medications so I knew perfectly well how they worked and the effect they would have on me. I could barely keep my eyes open that evening.

The next morning, it became clear to me that I no longer had my breast. It was hard looking in the mirror Each time I saw the bandages I felt a sharp pain in my heart. It was something I had to live with for the rest of my life. It was going to be difficult but I had to tell myself that it was replaceable. The ones that I lost were going to be replaced with newer ones. Alton did not show any negative reaction to me losing my breasts. He promised from the day that I was diagnosed that he was going to be at my side with his love and support. I was instructed not to lift anything over five pounds and to do absolutely no stretching or bending. I was not my normal self. I felt weak when I tried to walk. This surgery had taken a lot out of me compared to the other three which I had in the past. I needed a companion at all times to help prepare and serve my meals. I was happy when my friends from church came over to help with laundry and light meals. Some came over early in the morning to help with my personal hygiene because I could not do much standing. I was very grateful for their help.

On the day of the follow up, the plastic surgeon removed the big bandages along with one of the drainage bags and said that it looked good. He scheduled an appointment for the next week. He said that on the next visit that he would remove the remaining bandages and drainage bag. I waited until I got home to look at the exposed area. As I stood in front of the mirror I became slowly afraid yet curious to look at the area where the surgery was performed. To my surprise, I saw what I did not expect to see. I burst into tears with great emotions. I felt as if I was reliving the pain of cancer when I looked at my chest in the mirror and saw all of the scars. The area where my two breasts used to be, now looked like folded dough with numerous scars.

I was afraid for my husband to see my scars. In the area where the stitches had been, there were multiple cuts on my right breast and on the left was a huge one where both breasts were folded. The doctor said that they would unfold as soon as he started the treatment.

We were already in the winter season. Which was a good thing for me I could easily hide my flat chest by wearing a jacket. I was only allowed to wear blouses with button fronts because raising my hands would be difficult, and the only comfortable position for sleeping was on my back propped up with three pillows.

TRANSFORMATION

Six weeks after my mastectomy, I started my filling. On the first treatment, the nurse prepared a large syringe of sterile saline solution. Then she located the port under my skin, marked the breast areas and swabbed them with iodine to prevent any infections. The doctor came in and injected the tissue expander. I felt a little pressure while he was doing that because of the force which he used. Tissue expander are very hard so he had to use extra force during the procedure. On the other hand breast implants are much softer. Within minutes there was a rise in both breasts which I thought was very interesting. After the doctor was finished with the fillings he placed a small bandage on the puncture points. My next appointment would be in a week's time. I would have to go through this procedure for the next six to eight weeks. Week two came and I went for my fillings. Then came week three and that was when I started to feel great pain from the fillings. As soon as the doctor placed the sterile solutions into the expander, I felt an enormous amount of pain which I did not feel with the two fillings that I had done before. The pain was unbearable. The muscles in my chest went from being normal to feeling like I was carrying a heavy load on my chest. That was the strangest feeling of my experience but the doctor said that it would only last two to three days. Throughout my discomfort, I felt an expansion of what would be my new breasts. When I got home, I took care of the pain by taking a dosage of oxycodone. The pain lasted two days. I imagined myself going through that torment again. As the weeks went by the pain became so unbearable that my husband had to take me to my appointments because I was unable to travel alone. The tightness of my chest made me out of breath. I was gasping for breath at times which felt awkward.

By that time the expander had taken shape. Most days I would be in tears due to the pain. I wanted to stop all the procedures but I needed to keep my appointments in order to get to a 38C bra cup size. How could anyone go through such pain? After all that I had been through already it was beginning to feel as if life had not been fair to me. I was living on pain killers. They were my best friend because they kept all of the pain away. I was no longer sleeping in my bed because of the discomfort of lying down. Instead, I slept on a lazy boy chair which was in our living room.

We were finally in the last stage of the filling of the expander week seven. After that I would be able to do the exchange in a few weeks. It was the worst week of all. I felt like a mummy I could not move and the pain killers were not working this time. Walking took a lot out of me. I kept on saying to myself that after a few more days there would be no more pain and agony. However having to feel the actual discomfort was a complete disaster. When I got into the car Alton could tell that I was in great pain from my facial expression, so he did not bother to say much to me on my way home. I was happy that he respected my feelings although he kept asking ever so often if I was going to be alright.

The ride home took longer than usual because of the evening traffic. The first thing I thought about doing was reaching for the ox cyclone. I knew that after taking the first dose there would be relief from the pain and there was. I was able to relax with a cup of hot tea and a light meal. But in the middle of the night I was awakened by tremendous pain, again I took another dose of oxycodone

I got up early the following morning to take another dose of oxycodone in anticipation of pain. The only discomfort I felt at that time was the tightening of my chest which was normal at that stage of the process for two days, I fed myself with oxycodone. The pain was not severe because I did not allow the time period between each dose to expire. At the end of the week I was back to myself again which felt good. I kept on saying, "At last it is over. No more pain. I am free ".

In a week, I was back at the plastic surgeon's office for a follow up and the appointment for the surgery to remove the expander and put in permanent breast implants. The appointment that day went well as usual. The doctor said that there was no need for another saline solution and I was happy to hear that. Even if he wanted to, I would not have allowed him because of all the pain. I was ready to settle for the bra size which I now had. The appointment was scheduled to be in six weeks, allowing time for the healing process. The surgeon went through the procedure with me. He promised that it was going to be easier than the past and that there would only be two to three weeks of recovery. He also mentioned that it would be an out-patient surgery. I was excited for everything to be over so that I could see what my new breasts would really look like.

The nurse gave me all the pre-surgery instructions which included having a pretest done along with some minor preparations such as no eating after midnight before the day of the surgery. That was not at all new to me. I left the doctor's office with great satisfaction because everything seemed to be coming together. All of the appointments would be over with soon and there would be no need for me to be going into Manhattan on a regular basis. The surgery was scheduled for April 2012. I have not returned to work since the last surgery in October 2011. My husband and I had decided that I should take all the time I needed to fully regain my strength. All the doctors suggested the same thing because at that time I was in my fourth surgery and my body had not yet been healed thoroughly. Even if I did want to return to work, I couldn't because of my weekly appointments for the saline solutions and the pain that came with it would of kept me away from doing any daily activities that my job required. I would not have been able to work in that kind of distress.

The day for the permanent implants finally came. I was going to do the exchange from tissue expander to breast implants. My husband and I arrived at the NYC hospital, checked in and waited. Within minutes we were in the patient surgical waiting room talking with the plastic surgeon he went over all the necessary procedures. He also placed markings on both breast areas where he was going to perform the surgery. The wait was a little longer than it should have been because of the patient in front of me. I started to feel uncomfortable because we were already sitting there for over three hours but a nurse came by and apologized for the delay. Four o'clock that evening, I was escorted to the surgery room where the surgeon and his team were waiting for me. They all greeted me with a smile and said that I was going to be in good hands. I was used to the normal routine by then. I was talking to the doctor and the nurse when I was given the anesthesia. The next thing I remembered was waking up in the recovery room with my husband at my side. I stayed there for a few minutes, then I was ready to go home because I felt fine. There were bandages covering both areas of my swollen breasts but there was no pain at all. I felt perfectly normal compared to the past surgeries.

When we got home, I felt nauseous and had to run to the bathroom to let it all out. After that I was fine. I had a wonderful pain-free night. I was very surprised but happy from not having any kind of discomfort. The only evidence which indicated that I had a surgical procedure the day before was the swelling of my breast. I was doing my routine, making breakfast and walking around the house instead of lying in bed feeling sick and exhausted like before. There was to be no lifting of anything over five pounds during the recovery period.

As the days progressed I kept looking in the mirror but there was not much that I could have seen or felt because of the bandages. Although I was anxious to get a good look at what my new breasts looked like, I had to wait until my appointment with the doctor in a few days. Every day that I waited I became more impatient. Then it was that time. The moment had finally arrived where the bandages would be removed and my new breasts would be revealed. As the doctor slowly removed the big bandages he kept repeating "Looking good." I did not attempt to lower my head to get a view of what he was talking about. When he was through I looked in the mirror and for the first time I saw my new man- made breasts. They were not the ones I had grown with over the years but I was very happy with them. I was thankful to be given an opportunity which many women did not have because it was either too late, or they lived somewhere in the world where the technology is not available.

At the follow up, the doctor removed the bandages and I looked at my new reconstructed breasts and smiled. I now had something new that man had created. I kept on staring at both of my breasts. It is unbelievable what humans can do with their knowledge. My new breasts were firmer and more uplifted than the ones I had before. I left the doctor's office feeling very satisfied with the results and very confident about myself and my appearance. It was a relief for Alton and myself. All the surgeries were over with. The doctor said that as time goes by the implants would settle into a much better shape.

A few months have passed since I had my breast implants and I am very comfortable and happy with the decision I made. My new bra size is now 38C; before it was 38B. I am happy with the size although some of my friends said I should have gone bigger.

It has been four months since my last surgery and I feel perfectly fine like I used to before all of the surgeries. I am back to living my life as a happily married woman enjoying every gifted day that God has given to me. Sometimes, I reminisce about what I have been through and what could have happened if I had not taken the lump seriously when we first found it. I am happy to be alive and am taking each day one at a time. I take my health very seriously. I now have a different perspective on life and how it should be lived. Do not waste any precious time. Do all you can do while you are alive and healthy because without good health, we are nothing. It has been an experience for both my husband and I as well as for our family members. Fighting the battle of breast cancer brought us all closer together. We cherished everyone amongst us.

I now pray for every one of my family members and friends to be in good health. I have been through the storm of having cancer and I have made it through. I thank God everyday to be alive because I have a testimony and I can now use it to help others.

Many people may ask the question today "What is cancer?" Even some of the cancer victims do not have a clear definition of what is cancer and how it is formed. Cancers are alike in many ways yet they are extremely different in the way in which they grow. Cancer is a disease in which cells grow out of control. The cancer cells keep on growing and they continue to produce new cells. They override the normal cells and this is where the problem starts in the affected body part. Cancer cells can also spread to other parts of the body. When this happens, it is called metastasis. Some cancers tend to grow and spread very quickly; others grow more slowly. Most cancers form a lump that doctors call a tumor. Not all tumors (lumps) are cancerous. They have to be examined before they can be defined. Lumps that are not cancerous are called benign. Lumps that are cancerous are called malignant. There are other types of cancers such as leukemia that do not form tumors. They grow in the blood or in other cells of the body.

I am now in the remission stage. This is a period of time when the cancer is responding to treatment or is under control. In a complete remission, all the signs and symptoms of the disease tend to go away. It is also possible to have a partial remission in which the cancer shrinks but does not completely disappear. Remission can last anywhere from many weeks too many years. A complete remission may go on for years and can be considered a cure. Many cancer victims may think that it is impossible to still work and have a normal life during treatment. The answer is yes you can still work but may have to limit how much you do.

Some women do not show any signs or symptoms of having breast cancer in its early stage. That is why it is important for us to take our yearly screening before it is too late. Some of the signs that may indicate that you may be at risk of having breast cancer are a lump or thickening near the breast, or in the underarm area, changes in the size or shape of the breast, nipple discharge or tenderness. Also, if the nipple is pulled back into the breast or any change in the way the skin of your breast or nipple looks or feels (warm, swollen, red, and scaly). My advice to you is if you have any of these signs; please check with your physician immediately. Do not delay.

SPECIAL THANKS

First I want to thank the Almighty God my healer for bringing me through from such a horrible diagnosis without him I would have never made it through. Then I give special thanks to my wonderful husband, Alton, for being at my side from beginning to end. I thank you from the bottom of my heart for your love, patience and understanding. The cancer was very rough on you but you never left my side. I appreciate everything you did for me. I love you. May God bless you.

My daughter, Arisha, I thank you for being strong and believing in me. You are the type of daughter that any mother would most gladly want to have as her own. You encourage me with your words. You never one day broke down in sorrow thinking that I would lose my life over breast cancer. Instead, you were strong enough to encourage me. I love you my child, and I thank you for being such a wonderful daughter.

My mother, Eastlyn, I love you and I am extremely sorry for not including you from the beginning. However, when I finally told you the truth your love for me grew stronger than it was before. The way you love me now makes up for the times that you were not with me throughout my ordeal. I could not have asked for a better mother.

Thanks to my family, friends and pastors for their prayers and support. I love you all. You never gave up on me even when I had negative thoughts in the beginning. You kept the faith for me. You believed that I would have made it and I did. I thank you all for your love.

I dedicate this book to my brother who died in 2008 and to my father who died in 2010. I know that you both would be proud of me today for what I am doing with my life. You are looking down from heaven and smiling, "Yes, she did it." I miss you both very much. You will always be in my heart.

I thank you readers for taking the time to read my story. I hope that it did change your thoughts about cancer and its victims. If you have never been a victim of cancer, maybe you know someone who has and this book can bring inspiration. I came out of my diagnosis victorious and you most certainly can too. I love you and I thank you once again for your time. May God bless you and keep you and your family in perfect health.

To all the breast cancer victims, remember that we are all winners and overcomers in this drastic situation in which we fight for our lives. Whatever pain you are going through, remember that you are loved and you are never alone. There is someone out there who cares deeply for you and wants to help you in your fight. Do not isolate yourself from the people who are willing to help you and to stand and fight the battle with you because that is what it takes to be victorious. It takes more than one. Do not feel defeated by cancer. It can happen to anyone. Stand strong and know your rights. Cancel out all the negative thinking. It will only add misery to your life. All it takes is a positive attitude and a healthy mindset to be the winner. You will look back one day and say: I am in remission because I have won the battle over cancer. I wish you all the best of health in your battle with breast cancer.

www.ingramcontent.com/pod-product-compliance
Ingram Content Group UK Ltd.
Pitfield, Milton Keynes, MK11 3LW, UK
UKHW041954230426
12048UKWH00008B/341